Paranormal
KENT

Paranormal KENT

NEIL ARNOLD

The
History
Press

This book is dedicated to Joe Chester

First published 2010

The History Press
The Mill, Brimscombe Port
Stroud, Gloucestershire, GL5 2QG
www.thehistorypress.co.uk

ISBN 978 0 7524 5590 7

Typesetting and origination by The History Press
Printed in Great Britain
Manufacturing managed by Jellyfish Print Solutions Ltd

CONTENTS

ACKNOWLEDGEMENTS

I would like to thank the following people for their love, support, help and encouragement in writing this book. Firstly, The History Press, and my family – my dad Ron, my mum Paulene, and my sister Vicki. Also, my grandparents Ron and Win, and my girlfriend Jemma. Thanks also to Joe Chester, Sean Tudor, Terry Cameron, Marc Ruddy, Jonathan Downes and all at The Centre for Fortean Zoology, Jason Day, Adam Smith, Kevin Payne (for the research into Rochester), Karl Shuker, Nick Redfern, Jacqui Ford, Tom Atkinson, and all the newspapers I have worked with over the years. And many thanks to all of the witnesses who came forward to speak of their encounters.

NEW LIGHT ON OLD GHOSTS

Both the Romans and the Greeks give mention to Kention, making the county name of Kent the oldest recorded in Britain. The name derives from the Brythonic word *Cantus*, meaning 'rim' or 'border'. The county borders East Sussex, Surrey and Greater London. It's no surprise that this rural habitat is infested with ghosts – the area has been occupied since the Palaeolithic era. There are thousands of spectres, mentioned time and time again in various books. *Ghosts of Kent* by Peter Underwood, and Janet Cameron's *Haunted Kent*, being among the better guidebooks. There are also thousands of tales rarely recorded, whilst the more 'classic' stories, passed down through generations have become almost stale and dormant in their regurgitation. This chapter simply aims to shed some new light on a handful of Kent's most classic, haunted places, which over the years have emerged as personal favourites.

Queen of the road ghosts

Blue Bell Hill, a small village near Maidstone, is home to one of the greatest of British ghost stories. The setting is perfect for any eerie tale, for its Romanic roots, ancient structures – the village harbours Kit's Coty House (a Neolithic chambered tomb) and Little Kit's Coty (also known as the Countless Stones) – and foggy lanes exude a late-night menace. This is not merely a façade, reliant on atmosphere alone. In contemporary folklore, the urban legend known as the 'phantom hitchhiker' is popular worldwide. It is a campfire tale which sends a shiver down the spine – although in most cases it lacks depth. Similar cases across the world exist only as 'friend of a friend' tales, or what have become known as 'FOAF tales'. The 'phantom hitchhiker' tale is known in the majority of households and communities; a legend is all that it has become. However, the Blue Bell Hill phantom hitchhiker is

Blue Bell Hill village.

Kit's Coty House – a Neolithic chambered tomb.

a very different story. The stories reported are not mere exaggeration passed down through generations, and gradually altered to fit a specific stormy night. The Blue Bell Hill ghost story actually happened, but not as you've heard.

The classic hitchhiker legend is often told as follows: it's a dark night – sometimes it is raining – usually in the colder months. Someone, usually a male, is driving on a lonely stretch of road. Up ahead there appears to be someone standing by the side of the road, and as the motorist approaches he realises it's a woman. She is hoping to hitch a lift, but the driver can't help but consider it strange that an attractive young woman is on such a road at such a late hour. He pulls over. She looks pale and cold. She's only wearing a flimsy dress, or sometimes is clutching a small coat.

'Do you want a lift?' he asks through the partly wound-down window.

The woman doesn't answer but simply opens the rear door of the vehicle and glides into the backseat – or, less frequently, the passenger seat.

'Where do you want to be dropped off?' the driver asks.

In most versions, the woman gives an address. This address is not usually that far away, only within a few miles of the driver's own destination. The legend often mentions how the driver introduces himself, and to be polite strikes up a conversation. The passenger either a) remains silent, or b) says very little.

Not far from the destination of the passenger, the driver looks into his rear-view mirror, or casts a glance over his shoulder, and to his horror notices that the passenger is nowhere to be seen.

However, on the seat there lies the coat, or in some versions of the story, just a wet patch where the rain-soaked woman had been sitting.

The driver still heads for the address the woman gave, but remains confused as to where the woman has gone. It's very late at night, but he parks up outside the house and knocks on the door. The door is usually answered by an old woman or man.

'Can I help you?' says the owner of the house.

'I picked a girl up not far from here who gave me this address, but she seems to have vanished into thin air,' replies the motorist. 'She left this coat.' (Or, if an item of clothing wasn't left, the driver simply knocks to enquire about the girl.)

'You're not the first …' says the old man/woman.

And so begins the story of how the girl – invariably the daughter of the house owners – was killed many years ago in an accident, or murdered by a motorist, and now travels the highways and byways in search of her killer.

The phantom hitchhiker tale is a fascinating one. However, Blue Bell Hill's own road spirit is far stranger, to the extent that her presence on the hill has gained her the reputation, and honour, of being named the queen of the British road ghosts.

Just before midnight, on 8 November 1992, fifty-four-year-old motorist Ian Sharpe claimed he'd run over a woman near the Aylesford turn-off of the A229 at Blue Bell Hill. The Maidstone man first observed the woman on the outer lane of the dual carriageway, before she darted in front of his vehicle. As he hit her, her big round eyes bore into his. Mr Sharpe stopped his car but, upon looking underneath the vehicle and about the place, there was no sign of the woman. The witness told the police of the matter, who took his shaken disposition seriously despite the fact there was no body and no damage to the vehicle. The witness claimed that the woman appeared normal, with a roundish face, had fair, shoulder-length hair and was wearing a light-coloured coat with a blouse or roll-neck underneath.

A phantom hitchhiker. (Illustration by Adam Smith)

Two weeks later, on 22 November, a Chris Dawkins had a similarly terrifying encounter. Dawkins was travelling through Blue Bell Hill village, and just passing the Robin Hood Lane junction, when a woman wearing a red scarf ran out into the road. She quickly threw a glance at Dawkins before disappearing under the car. Fearing that the woman was trapped beneath his vehicle, the witness phoned his father from a nearby telephone box, who in turn phoned the police. When Dawkins' father turned up at the spot, his search for a body proved fruitless. So, just what was going on around Blue Bell Hill?

Researcher Sean Tudor – first introduced to the legend back in 1981 – got into the thick of the mystery, eventually uncovering a selection of similar incidents from the hill dating back a few decades. Several of these stories had been covered by the local press. Meanwhile, due to Sean's investigations, more witnesses were willing to come forward to speak of previously unreported encounters. For the press, a connection was brewing. In 1965, a fatal car accident had taken place on the hill. On 19 November, four young women, including a lady who was to be married the next day, were travelling up Blue Bell Hill when the car they were in, a Mark 1 Ford Cortina, collided with a Jaguar. Three of the women in the car, including the bride-to-be, died. The fourth was seriously injured, as was the Jaguar driver's passenger, who was discharged from hospital a few days after. Only the driver of the Jaguar emerged unscathed. Such was the horror of the crash that it made newspapers across the world.

The press, and the rumours, have always stated that the ghost girl on Blue Bell Hill is that of the bride-to-be, eager to get home. However, judging by the two reports involving

Chris Dawkins hit a ghost girl in 1992 and phoned his father from this telephone box near the crematorium.

In 1965, a fatal car accident occurred a few yards from this very spot at Blue Bell Hill.

Mr Sharpe and Mr Dawkins, there is no suggestion of a connection to the '65 crash. In fact, many accidents have occurred on Blue Bell Hill. This rural setting was sliced in 1972 by a dual carriageway, but the older routes, namely Lower Blue Bell Hill and Upper Blue Bell Hill, seem a world away from the roaring traffic.

It is no surprise that connections have been made between the accident and the haunting; they are the perfect ingredients for a local urban legend. However, the hill is a cauldron of mysteries, and does not just have one resident ghost.

Take, for instance, the case of Maurice Goodenough, who had a peculiar encounter in 1974 – nine years after the '65 accident. This was to be the first time that associations were drawn between the crash and the spirit. The *Evening Post* and *Kent Messenger* newspapers made the connection, which then seemed to embed itself in the minds of the general public, who would forever base what they knew of the legend on that fatal accident. Maurice Goodenough, a thirty-five-year-old bricklayer from Rochester, was driving on the A229 at around midnight on 13 July 1974, when he knocked a girl down with a terrible thud on the bonnet. On this occasion, the driver tended to the victim. She looked around ten years old and had brown, shoulder-length hair; she was wearing a white blouse, skirt and ankle socks. The girl had a cut on her forehead and grazed knees, and Mr Goodenough carried her to the roadside in his car blanket. The shocked witness could not flag down any passing vehicles, and so decided to leave the girl by the roadside and drive to Rochester police station to report the accident. Goodenough told police that the girl had mumbled the word 'Mummy' several times as she lay in his arms, but when he returned with the police they could find no trace of her. Despite a thorough combing of the nearby woods, it was as if the girl had vanished. The following morning, the police returned to the area with a tracker dog, but the animal picked up no scent and no other signs were found as the rain came down.

The incident was reported by the *News of the World*, and in the report the witness expressed his horror and confusion, but the press were quick to bring up the accident of 1965. The cases involving Goodenough, Dawkins and Sharpe bear similarity in that all three motorists knocked down a female late at night around Blue Bell Hill. All three witnesses searched for a body (Goodenough's case varying, as he went back to search with the police), but whilst the press were quick to tie the Dawkins and Sharpe incidents in with the anniversary of the '65 crash, Goodenough's encounter took place during the summer and did not involve an adult.

On possibly the same night, a couple had a similar encounter driving near to where Goodenough had hit the girl. It was around 12.30–1 a.m. and they were travelling up the northbound carriageway of the A229 to visit their daughter. Suddenly the passenger noticed a figure up ahead run from the left-hand side into the road, where she turned to face the oncoming vehicle. Alerting her husband to the figure, the passenger saw that impact was imminent and yet her husband could see nobody there. Convinced that the car was going to strike somebody, the passenger grabbed the steering wheel; but no impact came. The terrified passenger told her daughter that the girl in the road was 'youngish' and had 'big eyes'.

A couple driving by the foot of the hill in 1984 or '85, at around 10.30 p.m., saw a girl step in front of the car. Braking hard to avoid her, the couple could not stop in time and they hit the figure. Instead of getting out of the car, the driver reversed, but there was no sign of the victim. Similarly to Goodenough's sighting, when describing the figure, the couple mentioned that she was around thirteen years old, wearing a light-coloured top, and had bare legs and white ankle socks.

Since the 1965 crash, Sean Tudor has recorded around twenty more strong cases pertaining to a spectre on Blue Bell Hill. The majority of these have taken place at night, during late autumn or winter. However, a pattern fails to emerge as there appear to be significant variations in the reports. A handful involve motorists hitting a woman; a couple involve a child. Then there are those which concern a hitchhiker – which brings us back to the classic urban legend observed all around the world – and then there are a few very unusual cases which involve an old crone on the hill (which will be touched upon shortly).

The ghostly legend of Blue Bell Hill has become such a traditional local tale that, quite often, upon bringing the story up, you'll find someone who knows someone who has a friend who hit, or picked up, that girl or woman. Perhaps someone will also comment, 'Oh yes, I know that story, my friend has a friend who saw a girl in a bridesmaid dress on the hill.' The bridesmaid dress, much like the hitchhiker itself, is simply one of those added details passed down through generations who, in turn, have passed on their frightful, slightly distorted version. Sean recorded that, 'Only one – the case of Mr Grant and companion (1967/8) – had the girl vanishing from the back seat.'

There are also two unrecorded tales from the hill. In the autumn of 1968, a Medway man who'd dismounted his bicycle was walking up the now disused slip-road from Blue Bell Hill, which runs alongside the derelict Upper Bell pub, onto Common Road, when from his left-hand side a woman emerged. Considering it was a cold, wet and blustery day, the witness was shocked that the woman only wore a flimsy dress. Her hair seemed matted across her face and she gazed intently at the man. She then passed him, and glided back into the undergrowth

The disused slip-road where a phantom girl has been witnessed, next to the Upper Bell public house.

and vanished. The witness mounted his cycle and rode home like the wind. In his report, he stated that maybe the spectre had expected a car to approach, like in so many other incidents. Somehow, the image of a ghost girl going under the wheels of a bike being pushed up the hill seems awfully absurd. During the mid-1970s, a Maidstone woman travelling down Blue Bell Hill during autumn, at around midnight, observed in the headlights, up ahead on the left-hand side, a female figure wearing a white gown. As the headlights picked the figure up, it vanished just 10ft away from the vehicle.

And what of sightings pre-1965? During the colder months of 1934, a male witness was confronted by a female form at around 11 p.m. in the area of the Lower Bell crossroads. On this occasion, however, the witness – who was driving a motorcycle – stopped his vehicle and the girl asked to be taken to Burham, which is just a few miles west of Blue Bell Hill. The man, who had just come from that direction, obliged and the girl hopped onto the pillion seat. He dropped the girl off at Church Street, but as he turned his motorcycle around to return home, he could see no trace of the girl.

It's clear that this weird incident has no ties to the 1965 crash which occurred thirty-one years later. However, the murder of one Emily Trigg could provide a hazy clue as to the identity of this particular girl.

Miss Trigg was a twenty-year-old resident of Blue Bell Hill who was murdered in 1916. Her body was found at Bridge Wood and she was laid to rest in Burham churchyard. Could it have been Miss Trigg who wished to be taken to Burham on that night in 1934?

As you can see, the Blue Bell Hill 'ghost' could well be several spirits, or local confusion combined with urban legend and press influence. There is no doubt that seemingly real encounters have taken place on stretches of the hill, making this one of the most compelling of unexplained mysteries. And the next case will send an even bigger shiver down your spine.

During the early hours of 6 January 1993, at 12.45 a.m., months after Sharpe and Dawkins' encounters, the Maiden family were confronted by a very sinister wraith. Malcolm Maiden was driving the vehicle and his wife Angela was in the passenger seat. In the back were the couple's daughter (who was fast asleep), Mrs Maiden's mother, and a friend of the family.

Travelling from Aylesford, Malcolm turned onto the Old Chatham Road, at the Lower Bell crossroads. Around 300 yards up the hill, Mrs Maiden spotted a figure which at first she took to be someone in fancy-dress. The figure was in an old-fashioned dress and bonnet, and started to walk across the road from right to left. Malcolm Maiden spotted the figure in the headlights and slowed the car, and it was then that the horror was realised.

Standing alongside the vehicle was a hag-like apparition with mouth agape. A hissing sound suddenly filled the car, as the hunched wraith glared at the carload. It had a yawning chasm of a mouth, beady black eyes, and clutched in its hand a spray of twigs which the figure shook threateningly at the car.

Malcolm pulled away from the figure in total panic; the apparition moved towards the kerb and seemed to vanish. The Maidens' daughter suddenly awoke, sensing a heavy, nasty atmosphere in the vehicle.

Angela Maiden told the press that she couldn't sleep for many nights after the incident. The family as a whole believed that this was no hoax, but something ghastly and malevolent. In fact, their story gained strength when an appeal from the local *Kent Today* newspaper provoked a response from another family, who claimed they'd seen possibly the same hag the night before in exactly the same spot.

Sean Tudor believes that Blue Bell Hill is a very special place. This kind of location is often called a 'window area' in the paranormal world. These are places – often rich in history – which emanate high levels of strangeness. Why? No one seems to know, but Sean's research goes a long way in investigating the various phenomena which seem to plague this location. Blue Bell Hill is a truly bizarre place.

The 'old hag' of Blue Bell Hill, as sketched by a local newspaper.

The lesser-known ghosts of Pluckley

If you acquired a pound coin for every legendary apparition sighted in the old Kentish village of Pluckley, which lies north-west of Ashford, then you'd be a poor person indeed. And yet, pick up the majority of books pertaining to British ghost lore and this place will be mentioned time and time again, and is in many cases described as one of the most haunted villages in the UK.

Pluckley – Kent's most haunted village?

Resident spooks here include the Watercress Woman of the Pinnock Stream – a gypsy crone in a bonnet, said to have accidentally set herself alight by way of too much spilled alcohol and the pipe she puffed; a phantom coach and horses, said to travel along the B2077 towards Maltman's Hill; a ghostly colonel at Parkwood – the colonel hanged himself from a nearby tree; a spectral highwayman, said to loiter around the aptly-named Fright Corner; a miller who haunts ground on the opposite side of the B2077 where a windmill used to sit; a monk at a building named Greystones on the Bethersden Road; a schoolmaster from Dicky Buss's Lane who was found hanging from a tree in the 1920s; the red lady of St Nicholas' Church; and two white ladies, one from St Nicholas' Church, the other said to appear at Surrenden Manor. There is also the screaming man – who is heard around the site of the old Brickworks – and there's even a section of woodland (Dering Woods) said to echo with screams. Meanwhile, there's a Devil's bush – it is said that if you dance around this bush three times then Lucifer will show himself – and the ghosts of the Black Horse pub, the Blacksmiths Arms (built in the fourteenth century and once known as the Spectre Inn!) and the phantom Tudor lady who glides through Rose Court.

Despite the seemingly abundant spirits and the amount of attention the village draws, especially around Halloween, sightings of such ghosts are certainly few and far between, becoming extremely scarce in the modern era. Local historian, Jackie Grebby, mentioned during a personal investigation that there were actually around eighty-five different spooks in the vicinity (quite an amount considering the human population of the village is around 1,000), and yet not many of these lesser-known ghosts are recorded.

And so, what of these seemingly unknown phantoms? Well, during the 1970s, a relation named Joe Chester visited the mist-enshrouded graves of the local church on a mini ghost hunt. Whilst there with his brother Albert, not only did Joe see a peculiar flash of light in the cemetery, but after taking several photographs of the crooked gravestones, in one particular

The Pinnock is said to be haunted by the Watercress Woman.

Greystones. Haunt of a phantom monk.

St Nicholas' churchyard is reputedly haunted by several ghosts.

'Fright Corner' – haunt of a highwayman and also the eerie 'Screaming Woods'.

The Blacksmiths Arms. Once very haunted tearooms.

Is this a ghost at Pluckley? A misty form can be seen in the centre of the picture.

picture two hands could clearly be seen resting on Joe's shoulders! In the churchyard, a small white dog has also been sighted but has rarely been reported. Albert had such an encounter. As he entered the place via the small gate from the roadside, a fleeting shape rushed across his path, causing him to leap with fright. The form was whitish and resembled a dog; it sped out of the gate and uphill into the darkness.

One Halloween during the 1970s, several students visited Pluckley and camped overnight in the churchyard. When the local reverend asked them if they had had any luck ghost-spotting, one replied, 'Nothing except a big white dog.' The reverend told them it must have been the local farmer's sheepdog, but when the farmer was approached, he said, 'No, my dog's too old and doesn't roam around there.' The church organist was quick to add that it must have been the phantom hound.

Local reverend John Pittock performed several local exorcisms in the 1970s. His first was regarding a whispering apparition which drove one woman to the verge of a nervous breakdown. He commented at the time, 'I certainly believe that there are good and evil influences at work in the village.'

A personal investigation at the Tea Rooms back in the 1990s revealed that the then owner, Gloria Atkins, had several spooks to speak of. She mentioned that there were supposedly several in her home, one being a cavalier, the other an old woman, although she'd observed neither. She also stated that it was not uncommon for recording equipment to malfunction whilst in the building and, on cue, this happened to a camera and camcorder, despite there being full power. Gloria's daughter, Estelle, had seen spirits. During the first year of living in the place, Estelle woke one night and was shocked to see a young boy standing at the end of the bed. She told paranormal programme, *The Why Files*, at the time:

> He was doing something with his hands in front of his face, and he couldn't have been much older than five. Then, shortly after, I altered my room around, and woke one night to see a woman in the room. When I blinked she vanished.

Electrics were unaccountably tampered with in the building, doors opened and shut independently, and furniture moved of its own accord. Similar incidents have taken place at the Black Horse public house on The Street, which runs through the village. The pub has changed hands many times, although it remains unclear just how many of these departures were down to the ghostly activity. During the 1990s, staff reported that a little girl, possibly named Jessie, was to blame for the disappearance of customers' garments, such as coats and scarves. When the Gambling family owned the premises, the landlady reported hearing footsteps upstairs; and their cleaner at the time, Jackie Oliver, claimed that whilst polishing the old fireplace, something unseen touched her on the shoulder. A figure was once seen by this fireplace, and cold spots and strange atmospheres had been recorded there for many decades.

Near the village railway station sits the rather creepy-looking Dering Arms, where poltergeist activity was once recorded. The family who occupied the residence often complained of being pushed by an invisible assailant. Also said to roam the Arms, is the ghost of an old woman wearing a bonnet. The Dering family, who owned some 50,000 acres of the Kent countryside, play a huge part in the history of the village. Jackie Grebby's *History of Pluckley*, an in-depth account of the village, is recommended reading for anyone who wishes to find out more about the family.

The Black Horse pub. Once a haven for paranormal activity.

The Dering Arms.

The aforementioned 'Screaming Woods' hold an amount of interest. Strange figures have been reported in the area – whether ghostly monks, cloaked highwaymen or hooded sorcerers we may never know, but it seems that the most likely source of the alleged screams which are said to emanate from the thickets may be vixens, or indeed the local 'big cat' (possibly a puma) which has been sighted for the last 500 years around Ashford. The puma is not technically a 'big cat' for it cannot roar, but it will emit a haunting scream which can travel for miles.

The spectral coach and horses which heads towards Maltman's Hill, and also along the stretch of the old Roman road, may well have company. Reports vary, suggesting that there is more than one phantom mode of transport in the area; there have been sightings of a two-wheeled cart drawn by just one horse, whereas the more commonly known apparition is a four-wheeled carriage drawn by a number of horses, which are often headless.

Jackie Grebby encountered a shade when she moved into her home in the village:

I was cleaning at the bottom of the stairs with an electric polisher. It was late. My husband was upstairs decorating. Suddenly I was overcome by a terrible feeling and I just knew there was somebody on the stairs behind me, and I could stay there no longer.

One afternoon, Jackie had another fright:

I have an office in the attic and I'm up there most days. It was around 3.30 p.m. and I heard someone come into the house, slam the door and ascend the stairs. My dog reacted as if someone was there also. On another occasion I was sitting at the table in the kitchen, facing the window, when a person, who looked a bit like a tramp, appeared directly outside. They were bending down as if to help themselves to water from the outside tap. It gave me a shock so I went straight outside but there was no sign of the person.

After her experience, Jackie heard of several sightings of a ghostly tramp walking around the village.

One of the eeriest encounters on Pluckley's pitch-black roads took place in 1984 and appeared in one of the local newspapers. Gina McCartney was driving home from Great Chart, near Pluckley, in her thirteen-year-old Hillman Imp car, and as she came around a bend at 35mph, the car died suddenly. A thick layer of fog descended upon the lane, blanketing the vehicle and sending a chill through her body. When Gina glanced at her rear-view mirror, she was terrified to see a face leering back – someone was in the back seat! Bravely, knowing she had to get home, Gina leapt out of the car and then, to her dismay, she noticed that she had a flat tyre on the passenger side. She got her jack from the boot, but as she began to attend to the tyre she noticed that it had somehow inflated back to normal! Certainly shaken, but thinking that tiredness must have led her to imagine the flat, Gina got back in the car. There was no sign of the other person and she was relieved when the vehicle started first time. At the time, she told a newspaper that the face she saw belonged to a man around thirty-five years old. When she reached home, she sat up all night speaking to her boyfriend about the incident. The next day, Gina had her car checked over to reveal no problems whatsoever.

What is clear about the supernatural structure of Pluckley, is that many of its known spirits have gradually faded from public view, and are now age-old tales that reappear not always as ghosts, but as anecdotes. However, such was their reputation in the past, that over time they have become part of the village history, an indelible stain upon the brickwork, the fields and local perception. Even if the likes of the schoolmaster, the screaming man or the Watercress Woman are never seen again, they will remain tattooed upon the residents' psyche. Unfortunately, such well-established apparitions may prevent 'new' spectres from revealing themselves; but, as you can see with this coverage, Pluckley hides many secrets within its thorny hedgerows and aged buildings. Only persistent reports, however, will enable spectres like the ghostly passenger and the graveyard hound to gain a place in the 'official' list of Pluckley manifestations.

Dover Castle ghouls

Described as the 'Key to England', Dover Castle, owned by English Heritage, could also be the key to an ethereal gateway, because for many years people have reported eerie apparitions at the place. Dover Castle has the largest of any keep in Britain. Its cold, stone walls could tell many a chilling tale, for beneath the castle, and deep within the White Cliffs, wind a network of tunnels. Originally built under Anglo-Saxon influence, the castle was once merely a fortress, but improvements were made on the arrival of William the Conqueror. King Henry II turned the castle into the medieval fortress we see today.

The tunnels of the castle were extended during the Napoleonic Wars, and these subterranean points also played a vital role in the Second World War. Now, Dover Castle keeps watch over

Dover Castle. One of Britain's most haunted locations.

the port like a weather-beaten yet proud guardian. It seems that individuals who perished there, or once patrolled the place, are either still keen to frequent its dark corners, or could well remain embedded in the fabric of the environment.

Even more interestingly, Dover Castle does not thrive on stagnant legends, but can boast of modern ghostly encounters. In 1990, a member of staff claimed to have come across a seventeenth-century cavalier one morning whilst she was cleaning a section of the keep. A decade previous, a soldier wearing a helmet and carrying a pike was observed in one of the tunnels. The male witness, also a member of staff, described how the figure walked through a wall. It is unsurprising that staff are the most likely to see phantoms, as they spend so much time in the castle. However, tourists drawn to the place for the history, and also the legends, have been known to have paranormal encounters.

In 1991, an American couple commended the staff on the chilling sound effects they had heard in some of the rooms. The member of staff was quick to deny the use of such effects, but the couple responded by saying they had heard screams and groans coming from some of the passageways. Around the same time, it was reported that a man in a long blue coat had been seen roaming the tunnels.

Ghosts of servicemen have been reported on numerous occasions. During the early 1990s, ITV's *Strange But True?* programme investigated the castle. Tour guide Leslie Simpson spoke of a peculiar incident that occurred whilst taking a group of people through the Defence Telecommunications Network Station. A woman in the audience, who almost fainted, told Leslie at the end of the tour that she had observed a man in naval uniform, who appeared at first to be tinkering with the equipment. The man then walked hastily towards the group, went through the barrier and headed straight for her. The terrified witness fell to her knees as the man passed through her.

In the same area, known as Hellfire Corner, another tour guide reported how a young girl had conversed with an invisible presence, and the girl's father had also seen the spirit. Both witnesses claimed that the ghost was a 'gent' named Bill Billings who had been killed whilst assembling an amplifier rack.

Despite the numerous reports, guide Philip Wyborn-Brown was quick to dismiss the activity, blaming it on natural atmospherics and over-active imaginations. Of course, Dover Castle has attracted many paranormal investigators over the years. Researcher Robin Laurence described how, during a three-night vigil, several members of his team experienced strange occurrences. Sue Nickolls and Keith Akers recorded a loud banging in a gloomy passageway during the early hours. Two other team members, including University of Kent master Chris Cherry, experienced similar banging noises and managed to film a door shaking.

In the King's Bedroom, the lower half of a man's body has been seen walking across the room. On the stairway of the keep, a woman in red has been seen loitering, and in the same area eerie sobbing noises have been heard. One very popular ghost is that of a drummer boy who has been heard thudding away for over 200 years. Some have suggested that the ghost is of fifteen-year-old Sean Flynn, who one night was sent to Dover on an errand, but was killed by two soldiers who believed the teenager had money in his possession.

More recently, in 2000, a Mr Nottingham, whilst on holiday in Kent, reported seeing the ghost of a nurse in one of the tunnels. Part of the tunnel complex was used as a hospital, and the woman the witness saw appeared to be straightening her uniform as if ready to begin

The haunted King's Bedroom.

work. During the same year, a couple from Kentucky, USA, reported being on a tour in a large room when the lights began to flicker, unnerving the tour guide. In 2003, a woman claimed to see a shadow glide into the operating theatre. In 2006, a Mrs Fraser claimed that whilst on a tour through the tunnels, a man dressed in Second World War uniform emerged from a metal doorway close by. No one else in the group saw the man. In 2004, a ghostly doctor was also seen in the area of the old hospital.

Whilst some witnesses may genuinely be susceptible to unnatural phenomena, we must not forget that Dover Castle is the kind of place where people expect things to happen. So many investigations have taken place there, including one from television's *Most Haunted* team, that it is no surprise that some people see things which aren't actually there. Creaks, bangs, moans and photographs of orb-like images do not always suggest the presence of paranormal activity. We must also remember that, for a couple of years now, several holographic images of varying figures, including a Second World War soldier, have been projected onto the walls throughout the castle as a re-enactment. However, a woman named Alaina, whilst commenting on the *Your County* website, stated (verbatim):

> In response to all of the people who claimed to have seen the tall, dark haired man in full army uniform (green) in one of the WW2 corridors, I would like to add my sighting of him to the list.

The underground Defence Station is haunted.

I visited Dover Castle (2004) and was walking through the underground tunnels when I walked past a corridor on my left, I looked in thinking it would be just like the rest and full of Second World War memorabilia but it wasn't. It was completely empty apart from a long chest of some sort on the right hand wall. Anyway, as soon as I looked into the closed off room/corridor a tall dark haired gentleman appeared to walk out of the closed door at the far end and close the door behind him (as I have said, the door was closed already). He was tall, over 6ft, with dark hair and was holding some papers in his hand.

What confused me though was the fact that he looked like some sort of projection or hologram, I have read a comment from somebody on the site who says that it is a hologram but I would like to ask this person to go and have another look and search for the equipment that should have been in the room to project the image onto the door. I looked for any equipment for some time as I thought that it was just another dramatisation by the castle 'trustees' but I can quite honestly say that I found no evidence of this man being a 'creation' of the castle.

Dover Castle seems to be a 'window' area, harbouring spirits that appear to act as nothing more than recordings, soaked into the beautiful history of the place.

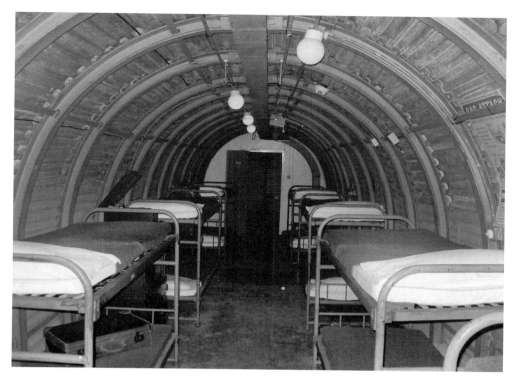

The underground hospital harbours several ghosts.

Haunted Rochester High Street

Rochester, a former antiquated city, is in the heart of the county of Kent – 'the Garden of England'. It no longer holds city status, although historically it was accorded its title along with Canterbury (which still holds its title). Rochester's best-known resident was Charles Dickens, who, although growing up around Chatham, is often connected to Rochester because, apart from London, it is the place most featured in his books. So it's no surprise that Dickens is the most famous local spirit. It is said that his ghost is annually (around Christmas) seen standing beneath the clock face of the Corn Exchange. However, after speaking to many local shop owners and residents, it seems that this once potent ghost tale is merely myth, for it seems that no one experiences Dickens anymore.

Take a tour through the High Street, from the Chatham end, and walk right through to the famous castle; you'll be delighted to find that Rochester harbours many unrecorded apparitions, which have been much ignored in books.

Beginning at Rochester railway station, you might spot the spectre of a suicide victim. The tale originates from more than a century ago, when a guard on board a late-night train from London to Medway checked in on a rather refined gentleman, who had told the guard earlier

Rochester railway station.

that he would like to be notified when arriving at Rochester. To the utmost horror of the guard, upon entering the compartment he saw the man dying, sporting a bullet wound in his neck. The weapon used was lying next to the body. After being taken to St Bartholomew's Hospital, the man died. After an inquest, Dr William Crewe – who was a surgeon at Guy's Hospital in London – concluded it had been suicide. It is a mystery why the victim chose to kill himself in the historic city, so far from his home in Nottingham. Around two months after the incident, two porters described seeing the ghost of a gentleman standing on one of the platforms. The figure was holding its neck as if in pain, and vanished before the eyes of the witnesses.

Across the road from the station, on St Margaret's Bank, sits The Little Theatre, which up until 1958 was a warehouse. It is said to be haunted by a man in a wide-brimmed hat and long cloak. The apparition has been known to pester audience members.

Heading towards the cobbled part of Rochester will take the inquisitive traveller across the junction at Star Hill. Here sits the Royal Function Rooms (built in 1791 and beginning life as the Theatre Royal) which is flanked by Georgian houses. This building is nowadays hired for parties, but its stage remains the second oldest in England and has seen many a variety act perform. Three ghosts are said to haunt the building. One of these is an aggressive man, who has been seen running around the stage, knocking chairs over and causing chaos. He is said to be angered when the stage curtains are left drawn, and his displeasure is displayed when he runs

The Royal Function Rooms on Star Hill, Rochester.

behind the curtain and thumps it. The second ghost is also a phantom of some aggression – a man, who has often been heard shouting in the stage area. The most peaceful of the resident spooks is said to be a woman wearing a long dress and bonnet.

At the beginning of the High Street, on the right, sits the Queen Charlotte pub. Despite being one of the newer public houses, in comparison to some of the far more historic pubs on the street, it has two apparitions. Local researcher Kevin Payne commented that:

> During the First World War there proved to be several spies in Medway collaborating with the Germans. Several were caught, including the then landlord [of the Queen Charlotte] who, after closing time, would climb into the attic to send information to the enemy via transmitter.

A more recent landlord reported hearing strange tapping noises emanating from the attic, as well as shuffling noises. The other resident spook of the pub is said to be an elderly lady in grey, who likes to smash the occasional glass in the bar. Staff know she is present by the odour of lavender which permeates the room.

Crossing the road, the Dot Café, at No. 172, is an Internet café. Despite being a relatively new business, the building is very old, so it is no surprise that the past has left a residue. The kitchen upstairs is said to be haunted by an unseen ghost, which often leaves the staff feeling uneasy with their surroundings. Staff have been touched by the apparition and have also heard

The Queen Charlotte public house.

manly sighs. Cigarette smoke, an odour sensed in several High Street buildings, has often been recorded, and employees refuse to visit the kitchen alone.

Further along from the café are the Thai-For-Two Restaurant, at No. 151, and Holland & Barrett at No. 142. This shop used to be Reeves China Shop and then Julian Graves. Beneath Holland & Barrett, in the cellar, is a bricked-up tunnel which few seem aware of. In fact, many tunnels wind their way under the High Street – the majority of these are blocked off now, but many years ago they would have provided access to the castle a few hundred yards away. Legend has it that on this site, around a century ago, a young woman fell through a trapdoor and died. Staff often report seeing the woman in the cellar and also lurking around the shop. Eerily, the trapdoor is situated just inside the main door, close to the till, and is only erased from the modern furnishings by the carpet which conceals it.

The Thai-For-Two Restaurant used to be the Castle Tea Rooms, and many years before that the Edwin Harris Printer Shop. Actor Peter Cushing was said to frequent the Tea Rooms, and would travel there from his Whitstable home. Edwin Harris, born 16 July 1869, owned the shop as a thriving printer's and followed in his father's publishing footsteps. After his death, staff at the Tea Rooms often reported a ghostly visitor, a man dressed in black who would glide into the shop, disturbing the bell on the door. Many believed that Edwin Harris was the spirit, and his presence unnerved a good few employees to the extent that some resigned.

Opposite Holland & Barrett sits Eastgate House. It is without doubt one of the most attractive buildings in the street. Built around 1590, this Elizabethan building was the home of

Eastgate House.

Sir Peter Buck, an upstanding official of the Royal Navy and at one point Mayor of Rochester. The building has been used for many things – such as a boarding school for girls in the 1800s (when it was reported that an employee walked along a tunnel which was blocked by a skeleton resembling that of a horse or donkey). In 1897 it was acquired by the local council and turned into a museum, and it existed as such up until 1979 when the museum moved to the Guildhall further up the High Street. Several ghost hunts have taken place at Eastgate House, the most recent being in June 2009 when a five-hour investigation was conducted. The paranormal investigators charged the public £35 a head to look into the mysteries of the place, but the only evidence forthcoming was an 'orb' caught on film – although promoter and medium Donna Harris of the organisation Ghost Watch UK told the *Medway News*:

> While filming the promotional video, a heritage manager and myself heard sounds coming from one of the small rooms on the second floor. The noise could be best described as 'something falling' but the room was empty. The noise was clearly heard at two separate intervals during that day.

Eastgate House is mentioned in Dickens' *The Mystery of Edwin Drood* and *The Pickwick Papers*. The building now exists as a dedication to history, and it is said that, on occasion, a ghostly face has been seen peering from one of the upstairs windows. At the rear of the house sits Dickens' Swiss Chalet, which was presented to the author in 1864 by his friend Charles Fechter, a

Dickens' Swiss Chalet.

French actor. It was transported to Kent by boat and consisted of fifty-eight separate packages. The chalet, erected in Dickens' Higham residence at Gad's Hill, was used as a study and summer house until his death on 9 June 1870. It was then moved to London and returned to Kent, at Cobham, before being moved to its present site in 1961. There is a hazy legend pertaining to the chalet, which claims that Dickens has at times been seen sitting at his desk and peering through the shutters. Maybe he is still working on the unfinished *Edwin Drood*.

On the other side of the road sit two more haunted buildings. Elizabeth's of Eastgate is a fine French restaurant and Tudor building dating back to the sixteenth century. The restaurant is said to be haunted by an Irish sailor who sits at one of the tables, although the manager of the business remained sceptical when interviewed. The place is also haunted by a vague spirit said to be a woman, and behind the till there is an eerie reminder of times past, in the form of a child's shoe dating back several centuries. Meanwhile, the building next door, which was once the off-licence Threshers, has also seen its fair share of ghostly activity. The husband and wife team who currently run the shop have differing views regarding the activity, with Mervyn being a sceptic and his wife a firm believer. She commented in the spring of 2009, 'I have seen a grey lady upstairs around Christmas time, and in the attic have heard the sound of crying. It sounded as if a child around the age of nine was sobbing.'

On the corner of Crow Lane is Destiny's at No. 134 – a shop you would think should have a resident spook for it deals in all things mystical, from tarot cards to crystals. The building is

Eizabeth's of Eastgate.

Paranormal activity has been observed in this building, which was once Threshers.

actually very new, but it has two ghosts. One of these spirits is said to be a monk named Brother Peter. He loiters in the cellar, where there is a bricked-up tunnel, and is said to have perished when the foundations collapsed. There is documented evidence of this event and it seems as though the phantom is trapped in limbo. It is also said that a child haunts the shop.

Hardware shore Johnstone's is a family-run business. The store is haunted by a grey lady who often mischievously moves and hides items in the shop. On one occasion a priest was called in to exorcise the spirit, which only seemed to anger it.

The Six Poor Travellers House.

The Six Poor Travellers House was founded in 1563 by local MP Richard Watts. The house was used by travellers; as long as such tenants were not of roguish character, they were allowed to reside and then the following day would be given 4*d* (£1.75) to be on their way. Ghosts have haunted this building for more than two centuries and now the house is open to the public. The paranormal activity recorded often concerns eerie moans, possibly from those who died or were sick at the house.

Golding's Bakery also has a tea room at its rear. Here at No. 85 staff regularly get spooked by an unseen presence, perhaps because they know that this building was once used as a morgue. The cellar has been sealed up for many years and may well hide several sinister secrets, for it is believed that this gloomy basement was once used for autopsies! Meanwhile, Cheldgate House is said to be haunted by a bald man wearing a long coat.

Abdication House (Lloyds Bank) was occupied by King James II during the 1600s. This building has a secret trapdoor and hidden tunnel which was used by the King when he departed to France on 23 December 1668. Again, fleeting shadows have been reported and the unexplained moving of objects. Across the road, the HSBC bank, which sits alongside Black Boy Alley, is said to have a cellar which on occasion has a strong odour of cigarette smoke and the sound of a baby crying. The Dickens House Wine Emporium at No. 53 is a family-run business, and is known for its fine selection of wines and variety of Cuban cigars. In the upstairs room, a strong smell of cigarette smoke has been detected and footsteps are often

Golding's Bakery.

heard. Meanwhile, Topes, a modern European restaurant at No. 60, is said to have harboured a poltergeist and hag-like apparition in the past.

One of the most interesting buildings in the High Street is the Guildhall Museum, erected in 1687 to replace the original town hall. The building was gifted with some magnificent plaster ceilings and weathervane courtesy of Sir Cloudesley Shovell, who is said to haunt the place. Shovell was a distinguished Admiral of the Fleet and, in 1695, despite several warnings that his ships were way off course, he steered an entire fleet onto rocks near the Scilly Isles. Shovell was washed ashore, barely alive, where he was murdered by a local woman for his gold ring. Although eventually laid to rest at Westminster Abbey, Shovell's ghost is said to loiter around the museum, particularly on the red-carpeted stairs where on two occasions his spirit is said to have touched the shoulders of women working at the Guildhall. Strangely, not far from where Shovell's ghost appears, a portrait of him hangs.

If you fancy a quiet drink or a nice meal in Rochester, then the George Vaults bar is perfect. With four stunning floors, the highlight of the place is without doubt the fourteenth-century vault. Although the building has been severely revamped over the years, it is no surprise that the vault, which has retained all of its medieval architecture, is haunted. Staff have reported that the resident spirit is rather sinister, and has been known to spring from a crouching position to startle anyone who should be susceptible. Of course, the atmosphere of the place provides

The Guildhall Museum.

George Vaults.

a perfectly ghoulish backdrop for the ghost, which has also been seen crawling up the walls! Another apparition said to lurk in the vault is that of a monk.

The Royal Victoria & Bull Hotel sits opposite the Guildhall Museum and was referred to in *The Pickwick Papers* as the Bull Hotel. The building dates from the late eighteenth century, although an inn stood on the spot in 1555. It acquired its 'royal' title after Princess (later Queen) Victoria and her mother the Duchess of Kent stayed there to shelter from a storm in 1836. Paranormal activity, such as strange noises, litters the history of the place, and as recently as 2008 paranormal investigators visited the building. It is said that a room upstairs was once boarded up after a maid committed suicide.

And so we come to the castle and Rochester's most documented ghost. According to Kevin Payne:

> The most romantic ghost story of Rochester has to be that of the white lady (Blanche de Warren) who haunts the battlements. Simon de Montfort laid siege to the castle in 1264, and one of his knights, Gilbert de Clare, had begun to admire Lady Blanche de Warren, but his affections were rejected.

When Ralph de Capo hounded out the rebels, Gilbert de Clare slipped into the fortress and accosted Lady Blanche de Warren. Seeing this, Ralph (being a renowned archer) attempted to aid his lover by firing straight and true at her assailant. Despite hitting his intended target, the arrow glanced off Gilbert's armour and embedded itself in the breast of Lady Blanche. It is said that her forlorn form roams the battlements, pining for her lost love as she clutches that piercing arrow.

Rochester Castle harbours a romantic ghost tale.

Lady Blanche de Warren's ghost roams the battlements.

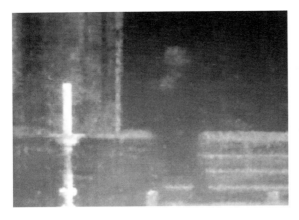

Strange figure at Rochester Cathedral. (Kevin Payne)

The castle moat, which has never housed any water, is where Charles Dickens wished to be laid to rest (although he was actually buried at Westminster Abbey). It is said that his ghost roams the area, although judging by the amount of graves there, the shadowy figure could be one of a variety of spirits. Duncan Livingstone, a local eccentric, was arrested for the murder of a young boy and was tried at the Guildhall, where he was found guilty. Livingstone was a violent man, especially when drunk, and it was during a drunken rage that he murdered his victim. He was hanged at the old cattle market on 3 February 1820, and his body was buried with haste beneath the castle walls. This was the last public hanging in Rochester.

Rochester Cathedral could well have a ghost or two. Footsteps have been heard on the hard floors, and during the festive season of 2008, fellow researcher Kevin Payne photographed a strange figure near the door. There was no one else around when Kevin took the picture, but on the print there appears to be a dark figure, mid-stride, standing around 50m away.

And that is your haunted guide to Rochester. Clearly a place littered with ghosts, many of which had not seen the light of day until now – and no doubt many more phantoms are waiting in the wings to rear their heads.

View of the cathedral from the castle.

2

KENTISH CROP CIRCLES

The world of the paranormal throws up many surprises; the seemingly modern mystery of crop circles is one of them. Unfortunately, in the modern climate, strange occurrences are often blamed on aliens. Peculiar craft whizzing through the sky? It must be aliens. The grisly discovery of stiff and mutilated cattle across the grasslands of the USA? Blame the aliens. Bizarre creatures in the local woods? Surely dumped here by the aliens. And, of course, the odd circular patterns and formations which appear in fields – aliens again?

According to the Medway Crop Circle website, crop circles have actually been around for more than a century. Of course, press interest really began during the 1990s, when all sorts of theories were put forward to explain such field formations. Sceptics believed that most of the patterns were attributable to clever pranksters, and this was certainly the case with a majority of designs. However, more complex patterns were blamed on everything from weird weather to animal mating habits.

Around 1918, it was recorded that a large circle appeared in fields close to Ashford. However, it wasn't for another thirty years that Kent became peppered with such sights. The Medway Crop Circle website commented, 'What appears to be quite odd about our early circles though, is the choice of canvas at times … oats, beans, grass, peas and oh yes, a circle in brussels sprouts in a Faversham field back in 1978!'

Most early crop circle designs displayed a simple circular pattern. During later years, such circles contained more circles within their circumference, or slightly differing patterns such as diamonds or triangles.

Despite the worldwide popularity of crop circles, unidentified flying objects and other mysteries – mainly due to the popular television programme *The X-Files* – in Kent fields during the 1990s, only a couple of circles were recorded each year. Although four formations were recorded in 1996, and six recorded from 1999, previous years had only seen one, two or three. A majority of the corn circles appeared throughout East Kent – no real mystery here when you consider that the eastern area of the county is extremely rural, and the rolling fields of Canterbury and Ashford are perfect places for such patterns to emerge. This isn't to say that other areas of Kent were ignored. A rough design appeared in 1992 in a wheat field at Swanscombe, not far from Dartford. And in 1994 rather vague circles were found at Istead Rise, near Gravesend – although it appears that the circles had in fact been constructed the previous year but had gone unnoticed.

By the latter part of the decade, the creators of these formations appeared to step up a gear with their designs. Several small, adjoined circles appeared in a field at Cuxton, and over the next few years more would turn up in the area. One resembled a dartboard, and others were almost bereft of circular patterns and instead appeared as series of lines, sharp points and futuristic emblems. Seven circular etchings were discovered at Birling, and a staggering twenty-eight appeared in a Y-formation near Cuxton. The pattern covered several hundred feet of land and baffled farmers who had once sneered at such creations. Researchers theorised that maybe the extraterrestrials were becoming more advanced with their messages, although the more down-to-Earth explanation was that the hoaxers who had constructed such designs were simply adding humour and deftness, and using more complex tools for their midnight escapades. One such fellow came forward to comment that, during the 1960s, as a child, he had come up with the idea of making crop formations, but experts estimated that it would take twenty men at least three weeks to construct some of the more complex designs. In most cases regarding the more intricate patterns, crop circles were discovered the morning after farmers had tended to their fields. In other words, such formations were impossible to create in one night under the cloak of darkness.

During early 2000, impressions resembling pyramids appeared in a field at Wouldham. Naturally, folklorists began looking for esoteric connections, with other enigmas such as ley-lines being thrown into the equation for good measure. During May 2000, a spectacular star-like formation appeared at Istead Rise. Were the extraterrestrial messengers pin-pointing Istead Rise as a window area for strange activity, or was it simply local hoaxers, adept at creating such patterns?

The year 2000 produced seven formations, with only one of these recorded from East Kent, at Dover. Whilst the intricacies of these designs were being admired, the belief in an alien connection was subsiding. Only the occasional report of strange lights seen in the vicinity of a circle, or witnesses who investigated the circles describing unusual feelings, added any mystery. The country had seemingly decided that there was no impending alien attack, or unearthly message, and if there was, it was certainly too difficult to fathom.

A few circles which were reported from Blue Bell Hill made the press, but then again, anything mysterious reported in that particular neck of the woods would raise an eyebrow. Again, connections with witchcraft and the paranormal were suggested, but were quickly dismissed.

Ashford was back on the map in 2002 having produced three circular designs. The following year, a pattern resembling the Star of David appeared in a field at Burham. An impressive flowering circle appeared on 26 July at Blue Bell Hill, within the vicinity of Kit's Coty House. In fact, over the next few years the areas of Burham, Borstal, Wouldham and Blue Bell Hill showed frequent activity. In 2005 there were four patterns: Blue Bell Hill, and the nearby Boxley featuring alongside two impressive designs at Meopham, near Gravesend. The same number of circles were produced in 2006, in Blue Bell Hill, Burham and Wouldham. One such design, described as a 'spectacular fractalised snowflake' by investigator Graham Tucker, was considered far too complex to have been the work of a hoaxer. So, just who or what had been etching such fantastic patterns in the local fields?

Crop circles have never been in the major league of world mysteries, mainly due to lack of thorough investigation. However, a closer look at some of the formations which have appeared over the years in Kent fields, prove that such patterns are not mere enigmatic flashes in the pan. Neither can such patterns completely be blamed on the dab hand of hoaxers. Corn circles examined in the mid-1990s revealed that the heads of the corn had been removed, twisted, or bent to create shapes such as triangles and squares.

At Thanington Without, near Canterbury, five circles (two measuring 47ft in diameter) appeared in 1996, despite only six being recorded that year by local investigators. An American biophysicist noted that the seed heads were completely normal outside the circle, but within they were devoid of seed. Such defects could suggest a more natural phenomenon, but this could not explain the feelings of immense relaxation that witnesses were experiencing once inside the framework of the formation. Andy Fowlds, a researcher into reports across Kent, commented:

Crop circles photographed at Burham, 2004. (Courtesy of Sean Tudor)

As far as my opinion on the circles go, I share the view along with other researchers that there is without question a genuine (non man-made) phenomenon taking place in the fields each year. There have been many cases where people have witnessed what can be best described as 'balls of light' both before and after the forming of these circles. I myself have witnessed and caught on film such unusual phenomena, both here in Kent and also in Wiltshire.

Sad to say there are also a number of man-made circles that various circle-making gangs across the country make each year – there have been a few in Medway over the years – we usually point them out when we go to photograph, film and document them.

In conclusion, if such circles are unearthly messages, constructed by supremely intelligent beings, then their signs are falling on deaf ears. The human race, despite methodical research, has not cracked the code, and in most cases such formations are not taken seriously by scientific research. The fact that the immense field patterns can only be observed clearly from the sky, could suggest that these 'messages' are not for us at all. Are intelligent life forms visiting in strange aerial craft, creating these impressions for other advanced beings? Have heavy objects made such indentations in the crops? Are spaceships whizzing through the skies and emblazoning

Are UFOs responsible for crop circles? (Courtesy of Alan Friswell)

their graffiti onto our fields via laser beams? Probably not. Yet, whilst the hoaxers continue to construct their own imitations, it seems that they are mere mites in this field of mystery. However, instead of looking to the stars for answers, maybe the solution to the puzzle had always been right under our noses, as some complex natural phenomenon not yet deciphered by the human race.

Watch that space …

3

MYSTERIOUS BEASTS

Sea serpents

Greatstone-on-Sea is a village on the east coast of the county, which sits close to the Cinque Port of New Romney. On 14 April 1998, two boys, Neil Savage and Peter Jennings, stumbled across the remains of a strange animal. The skull, a series of large vertebrae, and a mass of tissue, is all that was left of the creature. The carcass seemed to measure around 8ft in length and resembled a small sea serpent. The *Kentish Express* of 19 April reported that the boys mentioned their find to a neighbour, Mr Fender, who told the paper that the creature was, 'dark yellow, and has stripes running the length of it.'

He didn't believe that the beast was a conger eel as its spine appeared too thick. It seemed as though the carcass had been there for a while, as it gave off a rank odour. The newspaper, along with the *Folkestone Herald* (23 April), pictured the boys with their discovery. Fortean researcher, Paul Harris, sent the cuttings to zoologist Karl Shuker, who concluded that the creature was most certainly a basking shark – a fish which, when found decomposed on beaches, has often been confused with sea serpents. Shuker commented:

> All of the telltale features were present – the cotton reel-shaped vertebrae, the long triangular snout, and, most distinctive of all, a pair of slender curling 'antennae' projecting from the snout's base. These are in fact the rostral cartilages which, in life, raise up the shark's snout.

Several serpentine beasts have been observed in Kent's waterways.

In 1879, in a 'Letter to the Editor' in the periodical *Nature – The International Weekly Journal of Science*, Joseph Drew wrote:

> On Monday, 5 August, a number of geologists crossed in the Folkestone boat to Boulogne, to study the interesting formations of that neighbourhood, and, when about three or four miles from the French coast, one of these gentlemen suddenly exclaimed, 'Look at that extraordinary object passing across the bow of the steamer, about a mile or a mile and a half in advance of us!'
>
> On turning in this direction there was seen an immense serpent, apparently about a furlong in length, rushing furiously along at the rate of fifteen or twenty miles an hour; it was blackish in front and paler behind; its elongated body was fairly on the surface of the water, and it progressed with an undulating or quivering motion: *mirum erat spectaculum sane.*

Serpent sightings around the Kent coast are reasonably scarce. One of the earliest reports comes from 1912, when a Mr Stone and several other witnesses observed a 'long-necked seal' off St Margaret's Bay, near Dover. In 1950, at Cliftonville, between Margate and Broadstairs, a similar creature was seen by John Handley.

In 1999, a Mr Wire reported:

> I was fishing off Folkestone Pier with a fellow angler, when in the distance we saw a black object. I looked through my binoculars and saw a huge animal that I can only describe as a sea serpent. The creature was roughly one-hundred feet long and seemed to be diving and then resurfacing. We both watched it for about thirty minutes and it was so ridiculously large that I laughed and did not tell anyone else about it. The animal had a long neck, moved very slowly and looked all the world like the Loch Ness monster plesiosaur that people talk about. It was massive.

THE HERALD. THURSDAY, APRIL 23, 1998

MYSTERY: Peter Jennings and Neil Savage and the remains of the creature they found

TWO beachcombing boys found a "sea monster" as they walked on the beach at Greatstone on Tuesday.

Neil Savage and Peter Jennings, pictured, told neighbour Peter Fender, in Seaview Road, about their find.

Mr Fender said: "It's a bit of a mystery. The dead creature is about eight feet long, dark yellow, and has stripes running the length of it. The head is just a skull."

Mr Fender said it was too big, with a thick spine, to be a conger eel.

It is thought the body has been on the beach for a while.

It is falling apart, with the tail missing – and it smells.

Press coverage of the mystery carcass washed up at Greatstone-on-Sea in 1998. (Courtesy of Dr Karl Shuker)

River monsters

From the *Medway Messenger*, 7 July 2008, came the headline: 'Monster Mystery: Could there be something fishy going on in the river?'

Does the River Medway have its own Nessie? A strange creature has been spotted swimming against the tide near the Esplanade, Rochester. On Thursday, 3 July, the *Medway Messenger* newsroom received calls from Rochester residents who said they had seen the strange sight in the water. Some believed it was a pod of porpoises, but one woman thought she had spied a single animal.

She said: 'It was about 30ft-long, dark brown and mottled grey in colour. It was undulating like an eel and swimming towards Amadeus nightclub.'

The sighting is similar to descriptions of Scotland's famous Loch Ness monster. I can only assume that the witnesses did indeed see a large creature, possibly an eel, or misidentified several creatures together. Eels don't grow to 30ft in length, so maybe they saw a whale. Seals have been spotted locally but they do not reach such a length.

The River Medway flows for around seventy miles. It was originally named Medwege by the ancient Britons. Those born on the north of the river are referred to as Kentish Men / Maids, and those born in East Kent are said to be Men / Maids of Kent. Much of the river's serpentine form occurs in Kent, although it begins just inside the border of West Sussex and enters the

The River Medway.

Thames Estuary. The river allowed access for navigation around 250 years ago, and according to the Medway Council website:

> The deep, meandering estuary section is actually rather short, stretching only from the chalk hills of the North Downs to the coast. For tens of millions of years, when the land of Kent was part of a huge chalk dome, rivers like the Medway flowed north down the flanks of the dome. They gradually stripped away the surface of the dome, creating the landscape that we see today.

The biggest fish to have been caught in the Medway is the sturgeon. Specimens measuring almost 8ft in length were recorded from the 1700s. However, on Friday, 16 April 2009, the *Medway Messenger*, in their weekly column 'The Way We Were', written by Peter Cook, detailed the pursuit of a larger mystery river monster.

> Fishermen are well known for tales of 'the one that got away'. But arms cannot be stretched wide enough to describe the 'monster' chased by Tom Pocock and his sons Jack and Thomas junior. The tale was often told at The Old George, in Globe Lane, Chatham, which Tom Pocock kept until his death in 1947 at the age of 77. It was also a frequent topic debated in the New Inn, Chatham High Street, kept by Jack, and at the Three Brothers, another Chatham pub, kept by Thomas Junior.
>
> Before they became publicans, all three were fishermen, having served seven-year apprenticeships to become Freemen of the River Medway.
>
> The story goes that Jack Pocock was aboard his boat near Sun Pier (Chatham) one day, when he looked up to see a creature lying on the surface a few yards away. It was said to be about 40ft-long, and lying motionless 'like a monstrous eel'. The creature had a hump on its back and a long snout.
>
> Its colour was said to be 'greyish-white', the hair along its back resembling that of a hog. When Thomas Pocock senior arrived on the scene in his bawley boat, Thistle, he had with him a 12-bore shotgun, which he fired at the monster. But according to news reports at the time, 'he might as well have been firing an airgun at a battleship.'
>
> Next day he loaded the gun with ball bearings. A shot from this caused the creature to shudder and leap, but it got away. News of the monster reached the national newspapers. Soon crowds were congregating on the banks of the Medway in the hope of spotting it. A week after it was first spotted the creature broke the surface in Gillingham Reach, just under the bowsprit of Tom Pocock's boat. He had a big game gun with six inch cartridges, and got in a shot at Pinup Reach, but the creature dived and resurfaced out of range. Speculation was rife about what the creature could be. Some said it was a whale. Feeling unwelcome no doubt, it left the Medway and has never been seen since.

A fascinating tale indeed, and proof that such legends were not necessarily the product of over-active imaginations.

Meanwhile, during the 1980s, teenager Richard Mann had a terrifying encounter with a 'monster' in the Medway. He had been sitting on the flood defence wall at Strood, close to the Civic Centre, and decided to take a stroll down the steps to a muddy walkway, when suddenly

Rochester Bridge. A strange creature was observed near here during the 1980s.

he spotted a black, circular object at the foot of the steps. As the tide approached, the thing uncoiled itself and swam out into the water. Richard was so alarmed by the creature that he fled, and afterwards, every time he had to cross Rochester Bridge, he ran like the wind in case he saw the beast again – and this was indeed a beast. Richard believed the creature to be almost 30ft in length and resembling an eel or snake in form.

Could there really be monsters lurking in Kent's waterways, or are the sightings simply misidentifications of natural species such as whales? During the 1900s, the village of Wouldham had a rare visitor. The village website contains the following extract from *Kent – A Chronicle of the Century Vol 11*, by Bob Ogley:

> There was great excitement at Rectory Wharf, Wouldham, when the body of a narwhal arrived on the shore via the Medway. It is only the second example of the species to be washed ashore in this country in 500 years. The whale's body was taken to the Natural History Museum, in London. So, what is a narwhal? Narwhals are usually found in Arctic seas and rivers where they feed on cuttlefish, crustaceans and fish. The most unusual feature of the narwhal is that it has only two teeth in its upper jaw.

A Kentish dragon

Despite being relegated to the world of fantasy, alongside creatures like the unicorn, the dragon remains one of the most intriguing mythical beasts. In British folklore, more than 100 legends exist pertaining to fire-breathing beasts, almost suggesting that such creatures were real and not merely based on the fears of local men. Sussex, London and Essex all harbour tales of fearsome beasts, and Kent also has a few scant yarns referring to the existence of dragon-like forms. Were

Author Charles Igglesden wrote of a dragon-like beast at Cranbrook.

such scaled monsters the product of over-active imaginations, or actual recorded encounters with a creature that remains unknown?

Writer Charles Igglesden recorded the legend of a dragon from Cranbrook in his *A Saunter through Kent with Pen and Pencil* in 1906, stating:

> The magnificent wooded park of a hundred and fifty acres is richly watered by a huge lake, made in 1812, and a smaller one within the garden grounds, while further west is an old mill pond that rejoices in a curious legend. It is an old one, and the subject of it must be very ancient indeed, and as rare as it is horrible. Nothing less than a flying dragon is said to haunt the pond, but on certain or uncertain nights of the year it wings its flight over the park and pays a visit to the big lake yonder. But he always returns to the mill pond and it is said to pay special attention of a vicious kind to young men and women who have jilted their lovers. A legend with a moral is this. But a winged dragon! A dragon of the ordinary kind is bad enough, but a flying dragon! Augh! It is Mr Tomlin's opinion that there is stronger evidence of the existence of this dragon than of most of his kind, and of his fires having gone out in the closing years of the last century. Nothing short of this monster's malign influence could account for the curious fact that, till the coming of Mr Tomlin's eldest daughter, no child has been born at Angley for upwards of a hundred years.

Whilst it seems that many UK dragon legends originate from encounters with adders, and released reptiles, the Cranbrook dragon could well be one of the only tales to support the existence of a monster.

Big cats

For centuries, a strange and elusive animal has been roaming the UK, with Kent no exception to these wandering, cat-like creatures which, since the Roman invasion, have embedded themselves within the annals of folklore to present-day enigma. However, such urban myths,

Large exotic cats roam Kent.
The author has seen them.

which have become known as 'alien big cats', have become newspaper headlines on a frequent basis. The beasts remain confined to the murky realm of lore, where they are sectioned alongside vampires, werewolves and spirits, due to the lack of an official investigation into their existence, despite thousands of eyewitness sightings to back up their presence. In fact, such is the overwhelming evidence to suggest that the Kent countryside is home to a varying species of exotic felid, that such out-of-place animals should not be classed as a mystery at all. However, their existence has, over the last thirty or so years been only half-hinted – a murky photograph or a smudged paw-print – but the general public continue to see them.

There are three main species of cat alleged to roam Kent. Firstly, the black leopard, or 'panther'. What must be made clear here is that the term 'panther' is simply a word used to describe the melanistic leopard – a normal spotted leopard (*panthera pardus*) but with a dark pigment to its coat; a panther is not a separate species of cat. Although native to Africa and Asia, and rare even in parts of their natural terrain, they were once popular pets during the swinging '60s for London's high class and swaggering community, a general public adorned in fur, parading novelty pets on chains. These cats were often housed in a dingy basement or restricting garden, for all to see, and were commonly available from a visit to the pet shop or by way of a local newspaper advert. Measuring around 4–5ft in length with a very long, often hooked, tail, these muscular cats frequently outgrew their keepers, leaving many owners unsure of how to maintain such a large animal. The black leopard makes up for around 70 per cent of wild cat sightings in Kent today.

The black leopard is an agile, solitary predator that can weigh up to 170lbs. It is able to climb and stash prey high up in trees, and it kills with a bite, crushing the throat of its victim, often dislocating the neck – although one swipe of its claw can be just as lethal. When a black leopard kills, it kills to eat, devouring the soft parts of a variety of prey, often killing animals three to four times its own body weight, and tearing the flesh away cleanly, leaving behind a perfectly stripped carcass.

Secondly, the puma (*puma concolor*), the largest of the lesser cats, also known as mountain lion, catamount, painter and cougar, is native to parts of the USA, and has also been given the nickname the 'silver ghost' or 'shadow cat' due to its elusive nature. In some states, such as New Jersey, the cat has allegedly been wiped out, yet sightings still persist in the dense forests. In Florida (where it has become known as the semi-mythical Florida panther) and north into Canada, the cat, which is not a 'big cat' as it cannot roar, measures 4–5ft in length and weighs over 100lbs, standing over 2ft at the shoulder. The coat is fawn/tan-coloured, sometimes appearing silvery-grey; the young are spotted, but these markings generally fade as they mature. It has a long tail with a black tip, and white underbelly. The puma is also known as the 'panther' in America, just to confuse matters, and, for many years in Britain, sightings of black cats were blamed on black pumas. Black pumas have never been proven to exist.

The lynx is the third large cat which prowls Kent and much of the UK. It was native to these shores a few thousand years ago. Across the world the lynx is divided into four species within the genus: the Canadian lynx (*lynx canadensis*) inhabiting North America, the Eurasian lynx (*lynx lynx*) in parts of Europe, the Iberian lynx (*lynx pardinus*) critically endangered in countries such as Spain, and the bobcat (*lynx rufus*). They have short, stubby tails, large paws, large, tufted ears, and coats ranging in colour from rusty brown, red or yellow hues, and silvery-grey with mottled markings. Such animals can weigh up to 70lbs. The lynx feeds off a variety of prey, from rabbits to deer.

The beasts of Blue Bell Hill

In 1998, the Kent press created their own 'big cat' flap, albeit some forty years after the initial wave of country-wide sightings.

The Blue Bell Hill cat was described as a 'panther', or black leopard, and to newspapers such as the *Kent Today* it was a new mystery, especially after a flurry of sightings in 1998 around the wooded areas and grassy slopes. After a few months, even cat sightings across the river at Strood, and from the farthest corners of Kent, were being connected to the Blue Bell Hill beast! However, the press were several centuries too late.

The Pilgrims Way, an ancient pathway in the region of Boxley, is said to have once been haunted by a giant hound which has remained a rather obscure apparition embedded in the annals of local folklore. However, such a creature may well have been a flesh and blood exotic cat, if we go on anecdotal evidence.

The year was 1654 when the 'great dogg' [*sic*] was said to have savaged and killed a man, on what author Charles Igglesden wrote was 'the upper road'. Unfortunately, the reference in Igglesden's *A Saunter through Kent* is brief and vague. A similar marauding beast was said to have terrorised a church gathering during 1613 at Great Chart, near Ashford. The mysterious beast appeared during a terrific thunderstorm, injuring several people before disappearing. Of course, such yarns sound akin to supernatural fiction, but consider another sighting, this time in 1745 on the Pilgrims Way, when a peddler was killed by a 'lean, grey hound with prick't

Pilgrims Way has been haunted by strange creatures for several centuries.

ears', which at first appeared behind the man and his friend and then up ahead. The man is said to have been buried where he was mauled. Rumours suggested that the animal was a puma, for what dog has the ability to remain elusive in its behaviour in order to hunt and kill? What dog could hunt with stealth, and leap from trees?

Sometime during the 1800s, two men, including a Revd Edward who recorded the encounter, were walking near to Maidstone between Boxley and Burham when,

> at a point where the road ascends … in its course, we paused to take breath, and look't back and were surprised to see some distance behind us, and standing on the way we had come, a lean grey dog with upstanding ears … I was struck by its size … it appeared as big as a calf.

Was the animal merely a dog? Would these witnesses, even one as credible as a reverend, have recognised a slinking felid during a time when reports of such animals were rarely spoken of? In fact, a similar hound was said to prowl Trottiscliffe, near Gravesend, on another pathway that has produced several large cat sightings. Coincidence?

Fast-forwarding just over a century to the 1930s, teenager Leonard Cuckow and his friends were playing on the Burham Downs when they observed a panther that had possibly escaped from Maidstone Zoo, and was eventually tracked by more than sixty men. With rifles over their shoulders, they banged and clattered bits of metal to flush out the beast. The creature ran from cover and was shot dead.

View of the Downs from Blue Bell Hill picnic area. Enough cover to hide several large cats.

Personal investigations resulted in three sightings of a black leopard on the outskirts of the Medway Towns, in 2000 and 2008. In 1994, a black leopard was filmed by a Mr Eddie Dedman at Aylesford Priory. Slaughtered sheep were also examined, having been completely stripped clean and on occasion found high up in trees, stashed by an agile and powerful predator. Paw-print casts also proved that at least one black leopard was roaming around Medway, Maidstone and Sittingbourne.

Camcorder enthusiast captures big cat on video

MYSTERY OF PRIORY BEAST

DRAMATIC SHOT: Eddie is convinced that this is either a puma or panther

FILM EVIDENCE: Eddie Dedman says he has seen a big cat
Picture: ROGER JOHNSON

A CAMCORDER enthusiast claims that he has captured dramatic footage of a big cat strolling the grounds of a religious retreat in mid Kent.

By ROBERT BARMAN

In 1994 Eddie Dedman filmed a large, black cat at Aylesford Priory. The Kent Today *covered the story.*

The beasts of Bluewater

The so-called Bluewater 'big cat' hit the headlines as the new millennium dawned and millions of shoppers flocked to the new mall constructed at Greenhithe, situated between Dartford and Gravesend. Little did the general public know that long before the area was handbags and glad rags, large cats had been roaming the woods and fields – and still were, despite the shopping centre appearing right in the middle of their territory.

Reports of black leopard and puma sightings were reaching the press at a rapid rate. Several motorists had braked on the roads circling Bluewater in order to avoid nonchalant felidae sauntering across the dark lanes. The scenic pools, thickets and quarry sides were still being stalked by these large predators, and on a couple of occasions, from 2004 onwards, handfuls of late-night cinema goers had been spooked by large, slinking cats emerging from the undergrowth and prowling across one of the car parks. One large cat was even observed by a family on a Saturday morning, as they dined on their breakfast inside one of the food courts. They were amazed to see a large cat glaring back at them from the undergrowth, possibly eyeing up their meal!

For some, a Bluewater 'big cat' was too sensational, but the sightings continued. On 16 December 1905, London's *Daily Mail* newspaper reported on a mysterious predator said to have killed up to thirty sheep in the Gravesend area. Many local men searched the fields and woods but to no avail, and then the killings stopped. During the same year, *Farm & Home* of 16 March commented that between Tonbridge and Sevenoaks, several flocks of sheep had been attacked, many found on the verge of death after being disembowelled and showing damage

Bluewater, at Greenhithe. Haunt of both leopard and puma.

to the shoulder. However, folk who glimpsed the animal claimed it was dog-like, and so, on 1 March, a search party of some sixty men sought the beast, which was eventually shot by the gamekeeper of a Mr R.K. Hodgson. The animal turned out to be a jackal. *Blythe News* reported, on 14 March, that the jackal was on show at a Derbyshire taxidermist's, with the *Derby Mercury* adding, on the 15th, that the body of the creature was being exhibited by a Mr Hutchinson of London Road, Derby.

The stuffed Sevenoaks jackal, as it appeared on a postcard after it was shot dead in 1905.

Personal investigation resulted in a lynx being filmed around the marshes of Higham around 2002. A strange cat, possibly a jungle cat, had been filmed around lanes at Meopham in 2001, and each year over 200 eyewitnesses were coming forward to report their sightings. To this day, both pumas and black leopards have been sighted in Bean, close to Bluewater.

Other Kent cats

Naturally, when the local newspapers dig up an interesting story, they like to confine it to a certain area. However, large cats such as leopards and puma have territories of up to 100 square miles, so a cat roaming parts of Sevenoaks could easily wander into the neighbouring county of Sussex. And a large cat on the loose around Gravesend could find itself heading towards Dartford and further north. It is clear that there was more than one cat roaming Kent, and more than one species also. Large cats were reported with cubs, and many of the rural areas had their own beast. In fact, exotic cats have been reported from most parts of the county: in Ashford a black leopard was caught on film at Shadoxhurst, and paw-print casts were taken from Challock Forest; in Canterbury a local farmer lost more than forty sheep over the course of a decade to an unknown predator which killed unlike a dog; in Dover a cat resembling a serval was reported dead on the roadside in 2003; on the Isle of Sheppey a big, black cat was allegedly shot by a farmer on the marshes in 2001, and during the 1980s a local man kept a puma in a cage in his garden; in Thanet sightings of both puma and leopard date back to the 1940s; and in Sevenoaks a creature known as the Otford panther has roamed for several decades. Also, in January 1975, on the banks of the River Medway at East Peckham, angler Fred Lloyd got the shock of his life when a panther cub came tumbling out of the bushes towards him. The 2½ft-long cat hissed at Fred, whose instant reaction was to grab the felid and bundle it into his fishing box. He took the animal home and rang the RSPCA, who did not believe his story until an inspector visited Fred's home the following day. The cub is believed to have been Zar, a panther stolen from Colchester Zoo whilst en route to Surrey, but how the animal ended up in Kent we'll never know. Or maybe, just maybe, Fred had plucked from the woods evidence that large cats were living and breeding in Kent.

The most frustrating thing for the sceptics was seemingly the lack of evidence. They also wanted to know where all these cats had come from, what they were eating and why humans weren't being attacked. These questions can be answered with ease.

Firstly, a lot of the animals being seen in the countryside today are the offspring of pets which were purchased in great numbers during the 1960s and '70s, but were then released after the introduction of the Dangerous Wild Animals Act in 1976. Many people could not afford to

Sevenoaks had its 'Otford panther' legend during the late 1990s.

keep their animals, and numerous owners were turned away from local zoo parks – a majority of people therefore released their animals. However, these releases do not explain the older reports, from centuries previous. Such populations can be explained by travelling menageries and private zoos. Records clearly show that there were many travelling exhibitions working across the country. 'Beast shows' were not as reputable as the more respected exhibitors such as Barnum, and Bostock & Wombwell. Cats would no doubt have escaped into the countryside, and not many people would have come forward to admit to such an escapee.

Menageries were numerous across the country. Even the royals had a zoo at the Tower of London, where bears, leopards and lions were exhibited. Earlier than this, when the Romans settled here, they brought amphitheatres with them, which housed large cats. Again, any releases would not have been documented.

Of course, lions and tigers would not survive in the UK woods. Lions seek a pride, and both would hunt for larger prey such as humans. However, felidae such as leopards, pumas and lynxes would find the habitat of the UK perfect to survive in. The puma and lynx are used to the colder climes, whilst the prey in Britain is ideal for such animals. Rabbits, foxes, deer, livestock, rats, mice, squirrels, pheasants, and pigeons provide an ample restaurant. Why would a large cat, which has been born in the woods of Kent, hunt humans when there is easier prey to catch? Consider also that the leopard and puma are very shy, nocturnal and solitary animals. Sightings usually involve dog-walkers strolling through woodland paths, or motorists driving late at night on remote roads. The only time a large cat might attack a human would be if such an animal was cornered, provoked or injured. In the UK, such encounters are reasonably scarce, although at Gravesend, in 2002, a resident did claim he was scratched across his hand by a lynx after he cornered the animal to rescue a rabbit from its jaws.

Evidence does exist to support the notion that healthy populations of black leopard, puma and lynx inhabit the wilds of Britain. The problem is, lack of authoritative study means that such animals are certain to remain not only on the fringes of scientific enquiry, but on the outskirts of our belief. For comprehensive information visit: www.kentbigcats.blogspot.com or read the author's *Mystery Animals of the British Isles: Kent*.

The horror of Hythe

Hythe is a small, coastal market town situated between Dymchurch and Sandgate. Legendary paranormal author, John Keel, spoke of an incredible encounter at this location in his classic 1975 book, *Strange Creatures from Time and Space*, commenting:

> Four young people were walking home from a dance along a quiet country road near Sandling Park, Hythe, Kent. John Flaxton, 17, was the first to notice an unusually bright star moving directly overhead. They watched it with growing alarm as it descended and glided closer and closer to them. It seemed to hover and then dropped out of sight behind some nearby trees.
>
> 'I felt cold all over,' Flaxton recalled. He and his friends had seen enough. They started to run. The light bobbed into view again, and this time closer, floating about ten feet above the ground in a field some two-hundred feet from the panic-stricken quartet.

At Hythe in 1963, a weird, winged humanoid was observed.

'It was a bright and gold oval,' one of them reported. 'And when we moved, it moved. When we stopped, it stopped.'

When the light moved out of sight a peculiar figure emerged from the woods.

'It was the size of a human,' Mervyn Hutchinson, 18, told police later. 'But it didn't seem to have any head. There were huge wings on its back … like bat wings.'

Seventeen-year-old Keith Croucher saw a similar glowing object five nights later whilst strolling across a nearby football field on the Sandling Estate. Two nights after that a John McGoldrick and a friend decided to investigate the weird events and said they'd found an area of flattened grass where it looked as if a large, heavy craft had landed. The pair also found a set of footprints measuring two feet in length and nine inches across.

McGoldrick returned to the area with a newspaper reporter and they both allegedly had a sighting of a mysterious craft which illuminated the woods. However, after the initial fuss died down, there were no further reports of the light or the shuffling creature.

Bigfoot in Kent

Bigfoot is said to be a bipedal, hair-covered humanoid believed to exist in the dense woodlands of the Pacific Northwest of the United States. It may well have relations in the mountains of Asia, where it is known as Yeti or the Abominable Snowman. Reports exist the world over in the remote forests and mountainous regions which have rarely been explored by scientists. Yet, when reports emerge of similar man-beasts from woodlands of the UK, it is clear that we are not simply dealing with an unclassified creature, but a supernatural beast that we are never likely to understand. The UK has never been a natural habitat for primates. And yet there are a handful of reports, from Kent, involving seemingly genuine witnesses, pertaining to tall, muscular beings which seemingly cannot exist as flesh and blood forms in our woods. So what are they?

The more remote locations in Kent are still smothered by ancient woodlands and even forest area. It is unlikely that these vast areas could support an unknown species of ape, but they could hide esoteric secrets long forgotten by modern man. Legends of 'wild men of the woods', or the woodwose (Anglo-Saxon 'wudewasa') have existed through medieval Europe, and can be seen crafted into the framework of churches as leering forms peering from foliage. Across Europe, such wild men have appeared on heraldic coats-of-arms, and are said to symbolise our never-to-be-forgotten connections with nature. In some mythology, these figures are perceived as guardians or as demonic – but could such beings still exist in our local woodlands as nature spirits?

In 1974, a Medway woman named Maureen was making a fire in local woods at Walderslade with her boyfriend. It was a dark night and her partner was crouched, tending to the fire, when Maureen sensed a presence nearby. Turning to her right she was frozen with fear as she spotted two glowing, blinking eyes belonging to a hulking creature. It stood much taller than her and was only a few feet away. The creature appeared to be covered in hair, but Maureen could only see the muscular outline in the glow of the flickering fire. Too terrified to scream, she whispered to her boyfriend that she wanted to go home, and with that the humanoid lowered itself out of sight behind some foliage. Maureen didn't tell her tale to anyone for almost thirty years.

Walderslade Woods, where a hulking, hairy humanoid was sighted in 1974.

In 1992, Rochester man Kevin Payne had a similar encounter with a man-beast, this time in the woods surrounding Blue Bell Hill and Burham. He had been walking through the woods with friends when they became aware of two eyes up ahead on the pathway. As they neared the eyes, they all became unnerved and so decided to throw flints and sticks at the presence. All that the witnesses heard was the sound of their objects hitting the ground, as if the sticks had simply passed through the entity. Seconds later the eyes were gone. However, not to be deterred by the presence, the men continued on their way. Upon rounding a corner they met the eyes again, but this time they were just metres away, and clearly belonged to some kind of creature that was far taller than the witnesses. In terror, the men fled.

Kevin Payne and several friends witnessed a terrifying apparition in the woods near Blue Bell Hill in 1992.

Bizarrely, there seems to be an obscure legend from the area regarding a 'hairy man'. A lady, who now resides in Norfolk, got in touch to say that when she was a child in the 1960s, at Wouldham, near Blue Bell Hill, her grandmother used to tell her intriguing tales. One of these, allegedly dating back to the 1920s, was about the 'hairy man' of Wouldham, a humanoid often seen in local woods by children. It was completely covered in hair and the story had become embedded in her psyche. In 1997, when the local press (especially the *Kent Messenger*) were latching onto stories of sightings of 'big cats', one anonymous witness wrote in, on 5 December, to say that he had spotted a gorilla-like beast in the woods near Blue Bell Hill. Meanwhile, during the May of 1961, near Stone Cross at Ashford, two schoolgirls watched in horror as a hairy being emerged from woodland and stood, bipedal, in a nearby field. The form then scurried off towards the trees, but as it turned the girls said they noticed it had a tail.

If you think it is completely absurd to suggest that man-beasts are lurking in Kent woodlands, then consider the case of the astral ape of Sheppey. This particular creature was reported in *UFO Magazine* Volume 11, Issue 6, January/February 1993, as follows:

Whilst driving near the Kingsferry Bridge soon after 10.30 p.m. on 22 March 1979, six people called the police after saying they had seen an 'ape-like figure' dressed in silver, 'loping' towards the fence at the side of the road. Frank Roosien, one of the six witnesses, all of whom were in different vehicles, described it as having a one-piece suit, skin tight like a diver's outfit with no boots, belt, gloves or apparent openings: the face was not seen, though from his 'three-quarters rear view' there was suggestion of a visor. The figure was about five feet eight inches in height, appeared male and was stockily built. The head seemed 'like a tin can, flat on top, rounded with no neck'. In view of receiving so many calls the police quickly arrived on the scene, but by this time it had disappeared. Few of the witnesses could give any details as most were driving at around 40 mph at the time … a passenger in the back seat of one of the cars who had a better view said that his impression of the head was that it had a tube-like effect similar to that of the Michelin Man tyre advertisement. He said the figure turned its head to look at the car as it passed, and that the helmet came to a point and had a black rectangular shape across the position where the eyes would be, like that of a visor.

Strangely, *UFO Magazine* called this case 'A Space Ape?' yet the beast appears to have very few ape-like characteristics!

Even more surreal was the creature encountered in November 2008 by a young woman named Charlotte. She was heading towards the University of Kent at around 11 p.m. and was turning onto the Dover and Canterbury slip-road after the Dartford Bridge, when she observed something in the distance which was crossing this normally busy, but for some reason eerily quiet, stretch of road. It was on the opposite side of the motorway and was running with speed towards the slip-road. Charlotte approached the slip-road, and got to within a few metres of what she suddenly realised was a weird creature indeed. It stood over 6ft in height, walked on two legs, was completely black all over (Charlotte wasn't sure if this was short hair or a tight black body-suit) and had a pointed dome on its head. The arms and legs were very long and lanky in comparison to the torso, but what really spooked Charlotte was how the creature ran. She said, 'With each stride it took, the leg would bend and the bent knee reached all the way to the creature's face!'

This nightmarish humanoid had a strange, humped back also, and frightened Charlotte so much that her hands came off the steering wheel and she almost crashed. The being bounded into the woods.

Phantom hounds

Known as 'hellhounds', worldwide folklore speaks of these ghastly and fiery-eyed apparitions. They exist as possible omens of misfortune, even death, and are said to loiter around old churchyards and prowl dark, country lanes. They are usually black in colour and exude an air of malevolence – although they do not physically harm those they wish to accompany. The hellhounds are not the spirits of deceased pets, but instead calf-sized dogs said to walk through walls or explode into balls of flame. In the UK, the most popular hellhounds are Black Shuck, Padfoot, Stryker, and Guytrash. In Kent, phantom hounds are said to have walked the Pilgrims Way for a handful of centuries. Accounts of such beasts seem scarce in the modern era; their thunder appears to have been stolen by the array of large, elusive cats said to wander the

Phantom hounds, or 'hellhounds', are said to haunt Kent.

rural lanes. However, in 2001 a Mr Rick Flynn, whilst driving in the vicinity of Blue Bell Hill, had a nerve-shredding encounter with a ghost hound.

It was 10.35 p.m. on Monday 22 January. He had been to Bluewater and was heading towards the Medway Towns. It was a cold, wet and blustery night and, when he reached the foot-bridge near the Aylesford turn-off, a large, Alsatian-sized dog suddenly ran across the road ahead at great speed. It was whitish in colour. Rick braked hard, hoping not to hit the animal. The animal glided across the road, and seemingly into the path of a Mercedes Benz, and yet the creature eluded the vehicle and slipped through the barrier onto the Chatham-bound dual carriageway.

Mr Flynn was certain that the animal was of spectral nature. He reached home, sweating profusely; his hands were sticky where he had gripped the steering wheel so hard.

Bluewater shopping centre may attract thousands of people each day, but the dark lanes which surround the precinct attract something altogether more sinister. On two occasions, giant creatures resembling white wolves were observed, and on one of these occasions almost caused the witness to swerve their vehicle into a roadside ditch. The first encounter took place in September 2006 when a Mrs Whitmore was travelling with her husband from Bluewater at 1 a.m. As they took the A2 slip-road, they got the shock of their lives:

The woods surrounding Bluewater are prowled by two giant phantom wolf-like creatures.

Black dogs roam remote pathways. (Image created by Neil Arnold)

From the side of the café a few yards ahead emerged a huge, white animal which crossed the road slowly. As it reached the other side of the road it glanced back at us as we slowly drove by. It was terrifying. It was not a big cat or a dog, but something resembling a wolf – but stockier and bigger, and whitish-grey in colour. The animal had a snout like a German shepherd dog and large, pointed ears, one of which was darker in colour than the other.

On 25 May 2007, at 2.30 a.m., a woman named Zoe reported:

I narrowly missed a large, white canine, which looked like a wolf or husky dog, on the road leading onto the M2 coast-bound from Bluewater. I could see another [canine] in the distance. I think it's the old part of the A2. Lorries park up on the left and there's a truckers' café on the right. I saw the animal just before the café. It was the size of an Alsatian and looked fluffy like a husky. Friends and I thought it may have been an escaped guard dog, but the colour and the shape make me think otherwise.

Zoe's friend was in another vehicle, but saw no dogs in the road. Yet Zoe, eager to avoid hitting the creatures, and with fear building in her stomach, had swerved her car off the road. She thankfully avoided injury.

These two incidents echo a peculiar tale reported via the 'Your County' website:

My good friend recently stayed at a cottage in Dode, near Meopham, over the weekend. During the afternoon, whilst relaxing and admiring the view from his dwellings, he and his partner witnessed an unusual sight.

A white animal emerged from the woods at the side of a field, crossing about a quarter of a mile over the field and back again. Not that strange you might think, but apparently this happened in about twelve seconds! The animal looked as though it was after a group of rabbits and it ran faster than a horse. The action was more of a bounding than a run.

I enquired as to the size of this creature and was informed that it was much bigger than a dog, but not as large as a horse. In fact, a fox was witnessed passing through the same field and was minute in comparison. I am afraid that's it, no other clues are offered. I do not question my friend's authenticity one iota.

The village of Dode was wiped of its residents during the thirteenth century when the Black Death arrived. It remained uninhabited for fifteen years. The church is all that remains from the fourteenth century, and sits at the end of a 'no through road'. Some researchers believe the village to be cursed, and numerous apparitions have been seen in the area.

A phantom black hound was seen not far from Pluckley; witness James Sanderson reported the encounter via the website of paranormal magazine *Fortean Times*, stating:

About seven years ago [the late 1990s] I was still living in Kent in a town called Tenterden. Myself and three mates used to regularly drink in Smarden, which is just a few miles from Pluckley. The route we would drive home was a single-track back road, with the odd house and a few farms. We were driving back at about 11.45 p.m. on an October evening with patchy fog.

We reached the straight bit of road and ran into a thick bank of fog when a shape in the middle of the road forced us to slow down. A huge black dog was stood there, side on. If I had to guess I would say it was similar to a very thick-set Labrador. We had slowed to a walking pace, and then stopped. The car we were in was a Mini and it [the creature] was level with the window on the driver's side as it walked alongside us and towards the back of the car, at which point Jane, the driver, hit the gas!

In 1205, a vile beast was recorded by Abbot Ralph of Coggeshall:

In the holy night of John the Baptist, all night thunder roared and lightning, terrific, incessantly flashed all over England. A certain strange monster was struck by lightning at Maidstone, in Kent, where, in the highest degree, the most horrible thunder reverberated. This monster had the head of an ass, the belly of a human being, and other monstrous members and limbs of animals very unlike each other. Its black corpse was scorched and so intolerable a stench came from it that hardly anyone was able to go near it.

During the 1950s, folklore author Joan Forman encountered a black, phantasmal beast whilst residing at a school in the village of Goudhurst. She was spending the first few days of the summer holiday at the school alone, and at 3.30, during her second night there, she awoke to see a weird creature crouching by the bed. She said:

It was about two feet in length, I suppose, the size of a large cat or a small corgi. It resembled neither of these. It had a pair of huge nocturnal eyes like those of a lemur, and these were the clearest features of the apparition. I noticed them particularly because they were unwaveringly fixed on me. I think it was the most revolting gaze I have ever had to endure, for what emanated from the thing was an atmosphere of extreme malevolence and obscenity. With all its exudation of evil it was at the same time mocking. It stared at me for what seemed half an hour (although I suspect it was only a few minutes in chronological time) and I stared back, playing rabbit to its snake. I could not move to switch on the light, and in any case the creature itself seemed to emit some kind of glow in which I could see the shape of its face and head and the huge eyes, and a dim suggestion of the rest of its body.

After what seemed like an eerie eternity, the apparition gradually faded away, dispersing with the coming of the morning light.

Phantom hounds can allegedly represent good or evil. A benign spectre is said to haunt Leeds Castle, near Maidstone. During the fifteenth century, the Duchess of Gloucester (aunt of Henry VI) was said to have dabbled in witchcraft, and the first sightings of a black dog were attributed to such conjuration. Even so, the black dog of the castle saved the life of a resident, whilst she was sitting in one of the Tudor windows overlooking the moat. Wishing to stroke the dog, the lady moved from her position when suddenly the dog vanished. At the same moment, the bay she'd been perched in cracked, and the window area crumbled and crashed into the waters below.

Personal investigation revealed that two dogs in fact haunt the castle, both once being pets of Lady Baillie, who owned the castle during the 1900s. One of the ghost dogs is a large, black hound; the other is a small, white dog which has been heard scratching at doors.

Shurland Hall, on the Isle of Sheppey, was built between 1510 and 1518. Charles Igglesden wrote:

My informant is a lady who lived there, and, referring to the tradition that Shurland is haunted, says, 'Strangely enough I myself never had any fear, although no one else would stay in the hall at midnight in the dark. I had no fear either of the ghostly lady in the black silk or of the big black dog sometimes seen, or of the ringing of the bells from some unknown cause. Then there was the sound of the horse's hoofs outside the front door, and it was said that a hearse passed by. We would rush to the door and open it, but nothing was to be seen. All bedroom doors were locked at night, and any dog would whine if you tried to get him to pass into one of these rooms and absolutely refuse to enter. Door handles would keep turning, and fingers would run over the panels of the door. Huge hairy spiders infested the place, and it was always said that they foretold death. Outside at night, owls screeched and weird noises kept the inmates of the mansion awake, and it was difficult to persuade guests to stay.' There's a ghost story for you!

Phantom hounds have also been recorded in Chilham, near Canterbury, where such a beast is known as the Barrow Dog, and was seen in the 1940s. Meanwhile, a spectral hound is said to haunt an unspecified manor house at Willesborough, Ashford. However, the most terrifying black dog apparition occured near Cranbrook, and was again recorded by Igglesden:

Skull's Gate Farm lies just off the Cranbrook high road, and it is said that many years ago, an old man was murdered near here under revolting circumstances, and, what is more horrible, his ghost is still to be seen traversing the roadway. Why, I am told that only last winter a bicyclist says he distinctly saw the apparition following close behind his machine as he toiled up Skull's Gate Hill. And the shape of the ghost was remarkable – it had a long body like a dog, with four legs, but its head was human. How shocking!

The walking fir-cone & others

On 16 April 1954, at Dumpton Park, Ramsgate, Police Constable S. Bishop became a very credible witness to what can only be described as a 'walking fir-cone'! The creature, which ambled out of the bushes, was, 'covered in quills, having a long snout, a short tail, long claws [and was] Alsatian dog-size'. A peculiarity indeed. Just what was this strange creature, and why was it never seen again? Since the report, the case has never been fully investigated. Constable Bishop did what most witnesses would have done in the same situation – he called the police! There were no further reports of the beast, so had he observed some kind of ethereal critter, or simply an exotic pet – such as a porcupine – which had escaped? Consider also the case of the Hawkhurst 'bear', which was seen in 1983 by two brothers, eleven-year-old Mark and nine-year-old Peter. They were playing in their garden at Slip Mill Lane, at around 7.30 p.m., when they saw an unusual creature fall from a nearby tree. The boys were unnerved by the animal because they thought it was a bear. Police were called to the scene but their search found nothing except a few scratch marks on the bark. However, when the youngsters were

Is a wolverine on the loose in Gravesend?

questioned, they told the police, 'The animal was bigger than our dog [weighing 60lb] and covered in shaggy brown fur, and had long black claws.'

During early 2009, a peculiar set of footprints was found in a sandy, but frosty, bunker at Southern Valley Golf Course, Shorne, south of Gravesend. The prints were discovered by four golfers, and one of the men, a Mr Knowles, photographed the impressions. The prints, when compared to a size ten footprint, measured almost as long, and showed four claws on each 'paw', but an elongated heel. The prints were dismissed as belonging to a badger by a local badger expert, and the witness sent the images to Howletts Wild Animal Park, who told him that the impressions were probably made by a German shepherd dog! However, after looking through many sets of tracks, analysis revealed that the prints resembled those made by a wolverine, or another member of the mustelid family, the fisher! These animals are around 2–3ft in length, whilst the wolverine can reach up to 4ft. Mr Knowles mentioned that whatever had made the tracks walked on all fours, and was roughly 4ft in length, the indentations of the fore-paws being slightly smaller than the rear paws. The images were sent to zoologist Richard Freeman, who stated that a wolverine could well be the answer, and mentioned that although such animals have five claws, the fifth is not always evident in tracks.

There has been no further evidence of the mystery beast, and like so many other curious creatures from Kent, the critter has faded into local folklore.

The bat-winged monkey bird

This ghastly apparition was observed by a woman named Jacki, who reported it to the now defunct paranormal magazine *Beyond*. She wrote:

Back in 1969 I was four years old and travelling back from my auntie's house in London. Dad had been driving for about half an hour and we were going through the countryside. I was in the back of the car when I suddenly heard an awful, screeching scream. Mum and Dad were in the front chatting and heard nothing. It was twilight, and as I looked out of the back window into the trees, I saw what I could only describe as a monster. It had bat wings which it unfolded and stretched out before folding back up again, red eyes and a kind of monster monkey-face with a parrot's beak and was about three feet in height.

Jacki observed the creature again on 19 October 2006 from the bedroom of her Tunbridge Wells home.

4

ALIEN ABDUCTION

Unidentified flying objects, or UFOs, have been seen all over the world for thousands of years. Despite the growing interest in such a phenomenon, as a race we appear to be no closer to gaining any truth behind the mystery. Are these peculiar lights and silent objects the creation of the military? Are they nothing more than manifestations caused by public hysteria? Or, can all sightings be explained by natural phenomena, such as clouds, atmospherics, or man-made objects such as weather balloons and Chinese lanterns?

Kent, just like any other county, has its share of UFO folklore. Each year, hundreds of people come forward to report their sightings of strange lights in the sky, and Kent boasts one of the earliest recorded accounts of a strange flying object. In *Otia Imperialia*, the chronicle of Gervase of Tilbury, it is mentioned that a 'ship in the clouds' in 1211 dropped an anchor in a churchyard in Gravesend. Bizarrely, several men allegedly 'swam' down the cable which the anchor hung from, and hurriedly attempted to free the ship. The crew failed to free the anchor and so cut it loose, and the ship moved off into the night. A local blacksmith claimed he used the discarded anchor as an ornament for the church.

A UFO was reported over the Dover coast in 1913.

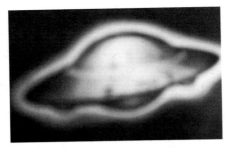

Most UFOs are described as saucer-shaped. (Image created by Neil Arnold)

The UFO craze did not hit the national headlines until the 1940s, when pilot Kenneth Arnold observed several saucer-like objects over Washington, USA. However, an 'Unknown Aircraft Over Dover' was recorded on 6 January 1913 by *The Times*. On 24 January, the *Standard* also reported that the unknown airship had been seen over Dover.

One of the most peculiar and terrifying UFO-related events took place a year previous at Sheerness. On 14 October, between 6.30 and 7 p.m., a weird buzzing noise was reported by several locals. Although aircraft had been tested on the Isle of Sheppey, this was an unfamiliar noise. At the time, there had been panic regarding sightings of airships, and the Sheerness residents started to fear that a German invader was hovering above, even though such machines had not ventured over Britain. The incident was certainly serious, as it was addressed by Winston Churchill in the House of Commons on 21 November.

The local press dubbed the incident, 'The Nightmare', for it was confirmed that the craft had 'not been one of ours', and yet it remained unconnected to any foreign enemy. Even stranger was the fact that lookout guards at Sheerness harbour, coastguards, local police on duty, and signalmen at Garrison Point, claimed to have seen nothing unusual. No British aircraft were in the vicinity that evening either, and when it was finally confirmed that the nearest Zeppelin airship was over 400 miles away, the 'Sheerness scare' hit the headlines. The mystery was never solved.

In 1927, at Upstreet, Canterbury, a man who was camping awoke in the night and observed strange balls of light bouncing on nearby apple trees. The globules of fire danced in the bellowing gales before disappearing.

Since these sporadic accounts, UFOs have been sighted more regularly across Kent, and since the 1950s hundreds of people have come forward to report their sightings. Of course, not every case turns out to be genuine. In 1967, a hoax was perpetrated by a group of students who strategically placed objects resembling UFOs across the country. Two of these craft were placed in Kent. The engineer apprentices from the Royal Aircraft Establishment in Farnborough were keen to play on the fact that 1967 had been a busy year for saucer sightings. One of the mysterious objects was situated on a golf course at Bromley, and another was discovered by members of the public at Sheppey. Naturally, the Ministry of Defence were quick to investigate the matter, but the whole incident was revealed as an elaborate hoax.

As with all mysteries, paranormal occurrences are preferably enjoyed at an arm's length, but when such enigmas infiltrate our homes, things become very serious. Although the suggestion of extraterrestrials visiting Earth has long been dismissed by scientists and sceptics, there are an alarming number of cases where innocent and seemingly genuine people claim to have been abducted by such invaders. The official line, of course, is that such events cannot possibly occur, but the next few cases suggest that something very strange has visited several people in the county, and plucked them from their beds.

In 1996, twenty-two-year-old Sally Walker had a series of peculiar experiences in North Kent. Prior to this, she was a complete sceptic regarding UFOs, although her husband Colin was a firm believer. Sally believed she was abducted by extraterrestrials over a three-week period, who left her with a strange bump on the back of her head. She felt that she had been given an implant during her second abduction, and after that she began to sketch strange alien beings and a barcode symbol with the figures X179, which she believed was her own individual code assigned to her by the visitors to her Gravesend home.

The first night it started, Sally recalled seeing a bright light and walking down a corridor to a queue of people. She then found herself in a large room full of lights, and the next moment she was lying on a bed and screaming, 'Why are you taking me?' to which her abductors replied, 'We take sceptics; you don't believe, we take you.'

When Sally was taken from her bed Colin was asleep, and he remembers no strange lights or visitations from peculiar beings. Colin awoke to Sally's voice saying, 'Are you awake? I've had a strange dream.'

Sally refused to believe what was going on at first, but the abductions became more frequent, and then they suddenly stopped; the beings have yet to return.

It could be said that some people are susceptible to paranormal experiences. Take, for instance, my relative Joe Chester, who has experienced many encounters with ghosts and UFOs over the years. During the early hours of one July morning in 1966, Joe's daughter Dawn, aged four, was taken from their home at Chatham. Joe had been fast asleep, as had Dawn and her sister Irene, aged eight.

Irene woke Joe, and through a veil of tears said, 'Dad! Wake up please, Dawn's gone!' Strangely, Joe felt reasonably calm, because he knew that the house had been securely locked so Dawn must have been either hiding, or awoken in the night and fallen asleep elsewhere after a wander. Of course, Joe was quick to check the bed first. No sign. Then he checked under the bed and in the cupboards, followed by an exhaustive search of every nook and cranny of the house. No sign. Joe's wife at the time, June, woke and joined the frantic search. All of the doors and windows in the house were still locked and, after half an hour, even the neighbours were called in to help. By this stage Joe was extremely worried and finally decided that the police had to be called. He headed for the phone box; however, after only a few steps outside the front door, he was amazed to hear a male voice in his right ear say, 'We have returned her.'

Joe yelled, 'She's back!' and ran back indoors. The family were stunned to see Dawn sitting up in bed, rubbing her eyes as if she had only just woken up. Joe lifted his daughter gently, keen to get information from her, but she could not say where she had been. For a whole day Dawn remained silent, and although she soon got back to her old self, she would never speak of that night again.

On 21 November 1990, a woman from Dartford named Maria woke up, lit a cigarette, and had an urge to approach the bedroom window. Looking out, she noticed an object in the sky which resembled a cartwheel; it appeared to be

Dawn Chester mysteriously vanished from her home in Chatham.

spinning. Her husband was away working and her son was asleep. She did not wish to disturb him. Maria walked out of the room and observed a ball of light in the hallway, and a voice told her to, 'Follow the light'. This she did, and she found herself downstairs and facing the front door. She was then instructed to pick the ball of light up, and suddenly she found herself being pulled towards an object outside. The next thing she knew, four beings were shuffling around her. They had large heads and big eyes. Maria found herself walking through a corridor, and then entering a small room where she was instructed to lie on a platform in the centre. Here, Maria was examined by a 5ft-tall white humanoid who inserted something into her ear and head. Her finger was pricked by an object, and she experienced a degree of pain until she began to envision a dusty world with two suns. Mud huts were situated on a horizon which appeared to be coloured orange and brown, but despite this being a seemingly alien environment, Maria felt it was familiar. Suddenly, Maria was back at home, ascending the stairs to her bedroom. Looking at the clock, she noticed that she had been gone for around forty-five minutes. Maria recalled:

> My feet were filthy and my night shirt was the wrong way around. I woke at 8.15 a.m. and found blood on the pillow, a mark behind my ear, and a bald spot on the back of my head. My nostrils were also caked in blood.

The cigarette Maria had lit was standing butt-end down on the table next to the front door.

Maria claimed that, on another occasion, she was abducted and shown a film of disasters taking place on Earth. She also photographed a strange aerial object over Bluewater Park, which would eventually become the site of the shopping precinct. Her house suffered unexplainable electrical problems, odd balls of light were also seen in the house, and she said that mysterious 'agents' once burst into her home and questioned her regarding whether she had received 'artefacts' from her abductors. Mail and telephone calls were also interfered with.

Slade Green, although in the London Borough of Bexley, is within the historic boundaries of Kent. On a warm day in July 1987, Jason Andrews was celebrating his fourth birthday with his family at their Slade Green cottage. Suddenly, the location was hit by a thunderstorm and flashes of lightning lit up the sky; but, more alarmingly, Jason began to mutter a series of numbers. These numbers turned into perplexing, complex equations which no four-year-old could have knowledge of, and the windows of the house began to shake as if an earthquake was ripping apart the countryside. Jason then calmly looked at his family and said, 'They're waiting for me. I have to go.'

Paul, Jason's father, reached for his son to stop him from walking out the door and into the rain. Despite a struggle, and the house shaking even more violently, Paul managed to pull his son not only from the door, but from the trance. The violent reverberations then abruptly ceased.

It wasn't until 1995 that Jason finally told his parents that strange beings had been coming into his room for the previous eight years and abducting him. A light would always appear first, and then a tall, spindly figure would materialise at the foot of the bed, accompanied by smaller humanoids. Jason recalled that in these nightmarish episodes, he could not move or speak. The figures would take Jason, against his will, to an operating theatre in a circular room with a metal floor.

Jason's mother, with Jean Ritchie, published a book on her son's experiences. *Abducted: The True Story of Alien Abduction*, tells of how Jason appeared to have been bestowed with remote viewing abilities, and how aliens had frequently monitored the property, along with alleged government agents. Sceptics have argued that the story is nothing more than manipulation by UFO investigators all too keen to pin-point the 'victim' as an abductee, instead of looking for a rational explanation – if there is one. Some would argue that Jason's tales originated from nothing more than childhood nightmares which were twisted into alien abduction.

Another young boy, named Carl, was allegedly abducted from his Sevenoaks home in 1994. His parents, William and Joan, described how strange noises were often heard at their Dartford home, and objects moved around the residence. Then Carl began to describe seeing little men with big eyes that had experimented on him with needles in a hospital. The family consulted child psychologists, but it was clear that Carl was being troubled by some sort of phenomenon, as he was sometimes left with strange marks on his body and a bloody nose. Carl's father worked late nights and so, in the hope of quashing the activity, Joan decided it would be best if Carl slept in her room. However, this did not prevent Carl from disappearing from the house – despite all the windows and doors being locked.

Peculiarly, other mysteries began to unfold in the area. The land which the family lived on was situated next to Ministry of Defence land, and on one occasion a calf, owned by the family, fell sick and died. Then another, and another. A vet was called to examine the carcasses, and men in protective clothing took the bodies away and claimed that they had been victims of salmonella. William was advised that no cattle should be farmed for at least twelve months, until a certificate of good health was administered. After a year, William contacted the Ministry of Agriculture and told them all about the visiting authorities, but the Ministry stated that they had no knowledge of such a visit.

Some theorists in the field argue that certain families are 'picked on' by aliens and subjected to all manner of absurd visitations and events. Others argue that such cases are nothing more than hallucination, or, in some cases, and rather more alarmingly, the work of the military or some kind of covert authority. Carl's mother claimed to have seen the alien beings, and also stated that her father and grandfather may have experienced night time visitations too. Had the family been chosen by those strange intruders, and were they simply continuing their clandestine activity with Carl?

No one has ever come close to explaining the phenomenon of alien abduction. Are the government, or some unknown body, really hiding behind the extraterrestrial guise to carry out undercover experiments? Have UFOs always been with us, and are their occupants, seemingly from distance planets, far closer than we think? The jury is out.

Alien abduction – myth or frighteningly real?
(Image created by Alan Friswell)

5
ZOMBIES!

Zombies, alongside vampires and werewolves, are figures of terror which have been sensationalised in movies for over 100 years. As an audience, we love these tales of suspense and horror because we know full well that such spectres and ghouls are confined to the television. Or are they?

There is a terrifying tale which originates from the marshes of Upchurch, concerning a fiendish creature known as the Bogman. This is a bogeyman rarely spoken of, a true monster from the closet who has emerged through Kentish folklore. Legend states that, during the early 1930s, a mummified corpse was discovered in a peat layer on the marshes. At the time, local police were investigating the disappearance of a schoolgirl, but instead unearthed the remains of a Neolithic hunter who, it was believed, had been murdered. However, the remains of the being provided a connection to the schoolgirl, as well as an incredible twist to the mystery, for it was said that a shoe belonging to the missing girl was found in the hand of the hunter! The police prised away the fingers to reveal a red sandal.

Several years later, it is said that the body of the girl was found by a local gamekeeper beneath a vegetable patch. Investigations revealed that one item of clothing was missing – one of the victim's red sandals! Some say that the gamekeeper was never questioned, and was poisoned by the girl's aunt.

Is the tale of the Upchurch Bogman merely a ghost story for cold nights by a campfire? Possibly. Mind you, it has been claimed that the remains of the Bogman were once housed at Rochester's Eastgate Museum (now Eastgate House). Some say that the Bogman rose from the dead, a zombie, and prowled a huge territory, ranging from the dank tunnels beneath Fort Amherst and Fort Pitt in Chatham, to the marshes. Such was the potency of the legend, that the fiend reportedly caused local hysteria around the time of the Second World War, and during the 1950s the spook was said to regularly attack local schoolgirls, who described being assailed by a mud-caked phantom.

Of course, the reality of the bog zombie is dubious to say the least. Descriptions of the monster vary, but one intriguing description states that the fiend, whilst on the roam, is always accompanied by two spectral hounds. Those who have heard of the undead creature claim that his head is almost hanging off, due to the fact he was sacrificially murdered by strangulation, or that his head sits atop his shoulders facing backwards. The Bogman may have a tattoo of a gallows on his left arm, and he may have bright red hair; no one knows how old he is or whether an exorcism was really performed on the marshes in the 1950s to rid the county of the spirit.

And what of the grotesque zombie encountered at Gladwish Wood, in Burwash, between Tunbridge Wells and East Sussex? In the September of 1956, Mr Arthur Warnford took his regular stroll through the delightful woodland but, as dusk began to hang in the air, he noticed an unsettling presence. Walking further into the wood, aided by his walking stick, he noticed how the birdsong had ceased, and the natural essence of the place seemed plagued by an overwhelming oppression and oddness. It was then that he heard it: the sound as if some animal, or possibly human, was trudging through the bracken towards him. He could spy no presence, but all of a sudden became disorientated in the surroundings he knew so well, and out of the gloom lumbered a figure which he could only describe as a zombie. The figure was limping, staggering, and from its mouth emitted a horrifying gurgle of desperation. Its clothes appeared tatty, the body reeking of the fumes from a grave – a musty odour which filled Arthur's nostrils as the figure approached. The thorns of vegetation clung to its scraggy form. Its arms appeared to spasm and jerk, and the face of the thing was merely a rotten skull, dusty and strewn with soil; its sockets were empty chasms.

The black holes of the skull seemed to seek Arthur out among the foliage. And, as that yawning mouth and those scrawny, decomposed arms reached for him, Arthur whipped his walking cane over the head of the loathsome spectre.

Zombie! (Image created by Neil Arnold)

Arthur awoke on the ground, immediately springing to his feet ready to counter another attack by the zombie. Yet there was no sign of the fiend and the countryside around him seemed to once again flutter with the sounds of nature. Just what had Arthur encountered in that thicket? Although this case has remained relatively obscure, some have put forward a theory that Mr Warnford was attacked by the ghost of David Leany, a man wrongly convicted of murder who was hanged in the area in 1825. Before his death, the accused vowed to get revenge on those who had wronged him.

6

WITCHES IN THE WEALD

There has always been something endearing yet spooky about the figure of the witch. Each year on All Hallows' Eve, children adorn themselves in witches' garb and take to the streets in search of candy from those residents kind enough to answer to their knockings. Of course, the word 'witchcraft' might send shivers down the spines of the naïve. Author Paul Devereux, in his *Haunted Land*, wrote:

> Witchcraft was for a long time not a favoured topic for the attention of modern scholarship. Then in the last few decades of the twentieth century it suddenly became very popular. The actual nature of mediaeval witchcraft was cause for argument and debate. Most modern scholars dismissed it as delusion and superstition.

It is a misunderstood term which conjures up images of voodoo and curses, but concerns neither of these.

Such tales are numerous and widespread but are rarely interpreted in correct fashion. Take for instance the Kent Online story of 2 March 2009, with the heading: 'Skeleton of village "witch" to be re-buried.' Now, for many people such a headline screams Hammer horror Gothic drama, and evokes images of sinister maidens sought by the local constabulary for liaisons with demons and the like. Of course, this could not be farther from the truth. The article continues:

Witchcraft – a misunderstood practice. (Courtesy of Alan Friswell)

The medieval remains of a teenage girl who may have been suspected of witchcraft are to be given a Christian burial and funeral.

The skeleton, found by Faversham archaeologist Dr Paul Wilkinson, is thought to be from the fourteenth or fifteenth century. It was found in unconsecrated ground under a holly tree, next to Hoo St Werburgh parish church, near Rochester. The remains would normally be left in archives for future archaeological reference, but the vicar of Hoo, the Rev Andy Harding, has asked for the body to be returned so she can be re-buried in the church grounds.

Dr Wilkinson found the remains about six years ago after a dig requested by Simon Wright Homes, which they were obliged to perform before starting their development. When they found the remains, the girl's skull had been removed from the body and placed carefully beside it, meaning she may have either committed suicide or was suspected of being a witch or a criminal. He said he had taken part in one other excavation, in Thanet, where discovered skeletons were 'different'.

He said: 'The male and female there had been buried and their heads had been switched. She was buried facing east with her head very carefully placed beside her body.'

Pottery found in the area dates back to medieval times and so it is suspected the body, which is currently being held at the University of Kent, was from the same period. The bone structure of the skeleton indicates the remains are probably that of a female.

Mr Harding said: 'We believe she was an executed criminal and so was not given the rights everyone else is. One of the things she could have been executed for is being a witch. We just want to give her a funeral that she was denied at the time. At the end of the day, God will be our judge. She obviously came from Hoo so she will probably be buried close to the rest of her family.'

Dr Wilkinson added: 'It's interesting that she will be rescued from a cardboard box and her journey will be finished in a manner that was not allowed her when she was first buried. I actually think it is rather wonderful.'

The public funeral will be held at noon on Saturday 14 March.

Tragically, it appears that many of the so-called 'witches' of the past were simply executed for their 'paranormal gifts', such as mediumship or clairvoyance. Even today such talents are often frowned upon, but in medieval times to display such gifts was considered an act of evil. One of the best-known cases involved the Holy Maid of Kent, a classic tale of Kent folklore from the sixteenth century which centred upon a young girl from Aldington named Elizabeth Barton. This softly-spoken girl, whose family lived in a small cottage, was sent to work in the local scullery aged just ten. Whilst there she visited the church with several other servants, but failed to understand the service. Then, one day in 1525, Elizabeth shocked the family cook by telling her that she had been spoken to by Mary, the Mother of God, and that sad times were coming to England.

The cook would, of course, have none of this babbling and told Elizabeth to hush. However, fellow maids were intrigued by the teenage girl and her strange fantasies. Calmness personified, in tranquil tones Elizabeth told her audience of the messages she had been bestowed, and in turn the maids told their friends and family of Elizabeth's wondrous talent. Local parish priest, Richard Martin, soon heard of the young girl and began to believe in her holy words. And more priests from local areas came to visit Aldington, so Elizabeth was persuaded to enter the convent at Canterbury, where she thrived.

Unfortunately, rumours of the gift Elizabeth had spread like wildfire and soon she found herself as an exhibit, as people began to pay to hear her words. Then, one day in 1533, a young man visited Elizabeth and asked if she had any prophecy regarding the King, Henry VIII. She responded calmly that Henry VIII would die if he decided to divorce his wife Catherine of Aragon and marry Anne Boleyn. This was shocking news, and a few days after the visitation, soldiers came to Elizabeth's residence and took her away to London. Tragically, she, alongside her priests, were hanged at Tyburn in 1534 under the charge of treason, with news of Elizabeth's execution reaching Aldington several weeks later.

Sadly, in the past, many other females have suffered similar injustice for displaying their seemingly supernatural powers. During the excavation of the Sevenoaks bypass, a gruesome discovery was made at the crossroads of the Pilgrims Way and Old London Road. A female skeleton, with a stake driven through her rib-cage, suggested that the victim was thought to be a witch. Crossroads play a major part in medieval burials, and are junctions where in the past offerings have been made to appease resident gods and spirits. Author Paul Devereux wrote:

> Crossroads were considered important supernatural places in the night-side history of Old Europe … the list of haunted crossroads could extend indefinitely, and it could be that many of the ghostly traditions associated with them are folkloric re-workings of the former general superstitions associated with such places.

Even weirder, the bypass is also said to harbour a very disturbing ghost – that of another road! During March 1979, a female motorist stated that whilst driving in the area, the road she was travelling on actually vanished. Suddenly she found herself travelling towards other cars but managed to avoid a head-on collision.

Author John Harries wrote of a haunted crossroads in his book *The Ghost Hunter's Road Book*:

> Near the crossroads of the A253 from Ramsgate to the Canterbury Road, and the A266 going south from Margate, there used to be a burial ground and a gibbet, according to legend. At night a glowing light moves along the road, flickers across the junction and momentarily takes on the shape of a robed figure.

The *Kent on Sunday* newspaper, on 17 August 2003, ran the following article, entitled 'Day the Devil came down to Faversham':

> The first English legislation against witchcraft was enacted in 668 AD by Theodore, Archbishop of Canterbury, but it wasn't until the fifteenth century that countrywide witch hunts began in earnest. From 1400 to 1800 it's estimated that between 30,000 to 50,000 witches were executed by burning, hanging, strangulation or beheading … probably 20 per cent of trials involved male defendants but the brunt of the hysteria mostly fell upon women. Most defendants admitted their crimes following 'examination' – otherwise known as torture – despite the fact that it was expressly forbidden … three women were executed together in Faversham, six women hanged in Maidstone and one in Sandwich. The trial of Joan Williford, Joan Cariden

and Jane Hott at Faversham in 1645 before Robert Greenstreet, 'Major of Feversham' and other aldermen was largely a reading out of their confessions. Jane Hott, a widow, confessed.

'At first comming into the gaol she had spake very much to those that were apprehended before her, to confess if they were guilty: and stood to it very perversely that she was cleare of any such thing, and that if they put her in the water to try her she should certainly sink.' (A sign of innocence.)

'But when she was put into the water and it was apparent that she did flote upon the water, being taken forth, a gentleman to whom before she had so confidently spake, and with whom she offered to lay 20 shillings to one that she could not swim, asked her why she perswaded the others to confesse: to whom she answered that the Divell went with her all the way, and told her that she should sinke but when she was in the water he sat upon a crosse-beame and laughed at her.'

Joan Williford confessed that the devil had appeared to her in the shape of a dog, and bid her to forsake God and lean to him. She said the Devil promised her money and she had it to her she knew not whence, sometime one shilling, sometimes eight pennies. She called her Devil Bunne and said that Bunne had 'carried a Thomas Gardier out of a window, and fell', causing him injury and pain.

When she came to the place of execution she was asked if she thought she deserved death: to whom she answered that she did, and that all good people should take warning by her and not to suffer themselves to be deceived by the Devil, not for lucre, malice or any other thing else as she had done but to stick fact to God, for if she had not first forsaken God, then God would not have forsaken her.

The third defendant, Joan Cariden, said the Devil came to her in the shape of a black dog which crept into her bed and spoke to her in a mumbling language. The next night it came again and said if she would deny God he would revenge her of anyone who had done her ill, and she promised the Devil her soul. She also confessed that there had been a meeting at Goodwife Pantery's house but one of the women who should have been there failed to arrive, so instead 'the Divell sat at the upper end of the table'.

In the seventeenth century, witchcraft emerged in Maidstone when a 'witch' was supposed to have bewitched a fragile and innocent young maid, and at the trial the poor girl was said to have vomited a rancid mess of blood, pins and bent nails.

At Dungeness, it was thought that, during fierce storms, witches would gather on the blustery marshes and fly through the air on broomsticks over Dungeness Dyke. At Rolvenden, witches were said to steal Holy Water.

The Village Net website, whilst commenting on the Church of St Mary the Virgin, states:

The church has 8 bells, which date from 1819, and were made by Thomas Mears II of London. The clock on the north side of the tower dates from 1810, and bears the name 'Thomas Ollive of Cranbrook'. There are many unusual and attractive memorials to be seen in the churchyard. The War Memorial was designed by Sir Edwin Lutyens and was dedicated to the Archbishop of Canterbury on 11 November 1922.

The font stands at the western end of the South Aisle. It is of an uncommon shape, being hexagonal. It dates from the fourteenth century and is emblazoned with the arms of

Guldeforde and Culpepper. The wooden cover is eighteenth century. Part of the hasps for securing the font cover with a lock can be seen on two sides. This was for securing the Holy Water from being stolen by witches.

Even eerie manifestations have been blamed on dark sorcery. Take, for instance, the case of the phantom fox said to haunt the railway bridge at Faversham. Legend states that a local woman used to dabble in witchcraft, and by her side sat a hideous, evil beast which looked like a cross between a dog and a goat. Naturally, local hostile whispers soon caused a riot and the woman, along with her strange pet, were killed. Ever since then, a phantom fox has roamed the area and has often been connected with the use of witchcraft, although the links seem rather vague.

Author Charles Igglesden wrote of Wye, and its holy well near Brook Road, as the scene of strange occurrences. It is said that the waters of the well were blessed and that, on one occasion, a '... dropsical woman who drank the waters vomited two black toads, which changed into dogs and then asses – then vanished.'

Unfortunately, much of what is written about witchcraft is misinterpretation. Kevin Carlyon is a practising modern-day white witch, who has visited areas such as Blue Bell Hill and spreads the word on the good ways of Wicca, a worship of nature in which the elements are understood and no darkness filters through. Carlyon has performed ceremonies to protect nature's landmarks from vandals and so-called black magicians. Cleansing rituals, performed

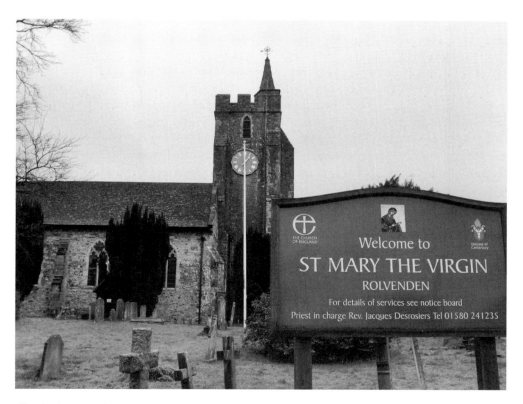

Church of St Mary the Virgin at Rolvenden.

by white covens, involve the use of flour, incense burners, an altar, and candles which invoke good spirits as guardians. Such a procedure took place when the Channel Tunnel Rail Link was constructed, in order to protect stones such as Kit's Coty House from disturbance. Legend has it that Kit's Coty House at Blue Bell Hill was formed by four witches on a dark and stormy night. Originally, three witches used their magic powers to lift the enormous capstone, but a fourth witch was required to help them finish the job. Again, much of what is written or believed about witches is misconception, but, as is often the case, legend overrides fact.

Interestingly, as mentioned in the first chapter, Blue Bell Hill also appears to be haunted by a witch-like crone who was seen in 1993. There was one rumour that a local hermit woman used to live in the woods, and was occasionally encountered by terrified individuals who bumped into her whilst they were out camping and she was collecting firewood. Legend is hazy regarding the woman, but some have mentioned that the crone spoke of how she guarded the hill. At the time of writing, locating such a local lady in archives has proved fruitless.

Even more eerie is the Blue Bell Hill legend spoken of by Maidstone man Tom Atkinson in 2009; he recalled the tale from his school days in the late 1980s.

Obviously we had all heard about the phantom hitchhiker on the hill and the endless re-tellings of this story sometimes led on to discussions about a particularly unpleasant old woman's ghost who was also rumoured to haunt the hill. The story was a bit vague but the gist of it was that she would walk next to the carriageway with a dog on a leash. When a car approached she would send the dog running out in front of the vehicle, causing it to swerve. Both the dog and the old bag would then vanish. I'm afraid I don't have any further details – it was just one of those vague rumours that circulate at school.

A terrifying tale indeed. In fact, it is no wonder that *Bizarre* magazine voted the village the strangest in Kent, with the *Medway Today*, of 4 May 2001, stating: 'Weird accolade for local haunt – a village in Medway has been named the weirdest in Kent.' The article continued:

Blue Bell Hill is the only place in the county listed in *Bizarre* magazine's 'Weird Britannia League'. The village was chosen because of the ghostly hitchhiker who appears and disappears as drivers approach. It is also home to the mysterious 'panther'-like animal known as the 'beast' of Blue Bell Hill. Kent came eleventh in *Bizarre's* league.

7

A MULTITUDE OF MYSTERIES

The flying jellyfish

To add more mystery to the Blue Bell Hill cauldron, *Kent Today*, 7 April 1999, ran the following story.

A motorist has told police she was followed along the M2 for nearly 15 miles by a mysterious flying object that hovered above her car. The woman was with her husband and a friend who also saw the UFO, which they reported when they arrived home at Gravesend.

The police said the woman driver, who has not been named, said the strange flying object followed them along the London-bound carriageway of the motorway from Faversham to Blue Bell Hill at Chatham where it disappeared. Police have so far been unable to find any explanation. Police spokesman PC Dave Wisdom said the driver described the object as transparent, with lights underneath which followed the car about 20ft from the ground. Checks were made with other areas and Maidstone police had also received reports about lights in the sky that evening. But it appears these were probably laser beam searchlights being used to advertise a town centre pub.

And so began the case of the flying jellyfish! UFO, monster, or something more down-to-Earth? The *Gazette & Times* of 14 April contained the following:

Motorists watched in wonder as they followed an unidentified flying object swirling around the night sky above the M2 motorway, from Faversham to the Medway Towns.

Two couples returning from the coast on Good Friday saw the object which they described as, '... like the bottom of a jelly-fish', circling close to their car, just past the Faversham turn-off.

Mrs Pauline Davis (51) had her attention drawn to the strange phenomena [*sic*] when her sister, Mrs Val Springhall, noticed the sky looked strange. Mrs Davis described it as being transparent, with white lights swirling around. The object disappeared, then reappeared about 20ft from the car. It eventually disappeared when the family reached Blue Bell Hill, near Chatham.

Mrs Davis, from Gravesend, said, 'I was dozing off when my sister said she saw it in the sky. When I looked I knew I had never seen anything like it before. A lorry in front of us was swerving all over the road, so I think he may have seen it too. It just kept swirling like the

In 1999, Faversham, Sittingbourne and Blue Bell Hill were visited by a 'flying jellyfish'!

bottom of a jelly-fish. You couldn't see an object, just lights. We called the police when we got home and they said there was a light show at Detling, but when we went back along the motorway there was nothing. If there is a simple explanation for what we saw, I wish someone would tell me.'

On the same day, the *Kent Today* reported:

You can sleep safely in your beds – Medway may not have become a hotbed for paranormal activity after all. The source of an alleged UFO sighting over the M2 could have been a giant laser image from a nightclub in Maidstone, we can reveal.

Last week we told you how a motorist claimed to have travelled 15 miles between Faversham and Blue Bell Hill with a mysterious flying object hovering above her car on Good Friday.

Valerie Springhall and her sister Pauline Davis were terrified when what they described as a 50ft long jellyfish-shaped object appeared to deliberately keep them under observation.

'I was absolutely terrified' said Mrs Springhall. 'I have never seen anything like it before in my life and I don't want to repeat the experience. It was around 50ft long, fluorescent white, and changing shape from round to oval as it revolved. At one stage it tipped over slightly as we could see small fluorescent circles in its main body.'

But the answer may be the laser lights emanating from Atomics nightclub in Maidstone town centre.

Sean Tudor, who writes articles on spooky happenings in the Blue Bell Hill area, believes lights from the nightclub laser show are capable of shining across large distances and is the most likely explanation for the sighting.

He said, 'My girlfriend and I happened to be out in Maidstone on Friday and saw the jellyfish display again swirling on the underside of the cloud cover over the town – which confirms to me that the UFO witnesses probably saw something like this the previous Friday. The display clearly has a powerful beam and would be seen for some distance which might extend as far as the M2 at Faversham but would, under the right conditions, almost certainly overplay the M2 closer to Blue Bell Hill. The reason it disappeared at Blue Bell Hill may have more to do with a confined arc the display travels than any sinister association. This doesn't definitely explain the story but the very close descriptive and behavioural similarities suggest strongly that this might be so.'

On 28 April, the *Gazette & Times* reported:

The UFO sighting over the M2 motorway on Good Friday was also seen in the hamlet of Bedmonton, near Wormshill. Mr Don Brown and his wife told the paper of their strange experience after reading the report two weeks ago, which they say described exactly what they saw. The couple were settling down for the evening on Good Friday when Mrs Brown noticed something in the sky. She called her husband who went out to look at the swirling object above.

UFOs seen over Medway in 1999 are believed to be nothing more than lights from a nightclub. (Image created by Neil Arnold)

He said, 'It was a clear night and there was nothing in the sky to suggest where the lights were coming from. It rotated from left to right in a three-quarter circular movement. It was there from 9.30 p.m. and it was still there when we went to bed at 10.30 p.m.'

The following day Mrs Brown asked her friends whether they had seen the swirling object but drew a blank. It was only when a friend told her about the report in the newspaper that the couple realised they had not been alone in what they saw. One explanation for what these and similar UFO sightings in the sky above Swale might be has been put forward by a local taxi driver. Carol Perry, who first witnessed the mysterious swirling lights in the sky two weeks ago whilst parked outside a fare's house in Roseleigh Road, Sittingbourne, believes they might be reflections on the sky of laser lights from a nightclub in Maidstone. A few days after the first sighting, Mrs Perry dropped off a fare at Maidstone and saw the lights emanating from Gabrielle's nightclub.

Hoofed horrors

The Pilgrims Way track, stretching 120 miles, runs across southern England from Winchester in the west to Canterbury in the east. It is no surprise that this route, once frequented by highwaymen, is extremely haunted. Judging by reports, it seems as if ghostly highwaymen and spectral coaches still patrol the dark stretch.

At Littlebourne Road in Canterbury, police were called out on several occasions after reports of a phantom horse. The local panic began when a Miss Dorothy Ramsay had an encounter whilst driving home late one night. She said, 'The horse seemed to fly up from the road like a great shadow. It landed on top of my sports car and smashed in the roof and windshield. After that it vanished.'

A handful of motorists came forward to say that they had seen the horse on the road and, as their vehicle was about to collide with the creature, it vanished on impact. One officer investigating the incidents commented, 'We don't want to start a ghost horse scare, but we have searched for the animal without success.'

Between Hollingbourne and Charing, the path which runs parallel with, and to the north of, the A20 from Maidstone to Ashford, is said to be haunted by a man on horseback. Some witnesses have heard the galloping of the horse but have seen no apparition, while on other occasions witnesses have reported seeing a large horse and rider rear up, but no sound being made by the agitated mammal. Even stranger, on occasion a rider has been seen passing along the Pilgrims Way and has spoken with witnesses. Those who are greeted by the rider only realise it is of a ghostly nature when man and horse suddenly vanish!

Some researchers believe that the ghost is of a man named Duppa, who once resided at Hollingbourne House. He was killed when he attempted, on horseback, to leap the wrought-iron gates of his property.

At Burham, near Maidstone, a spectral coach has been observed, although the occupants are never seen. Sightings have lessened over the years. Not far from Burham, at Aylesford, a fiery horse and rider are said to appear. During the 1970s, at Barming Woods, a horseman was reported crashing through the trees and even charging a vehicle. Meanwhile, at Farningham,

Burham. Haunt of a spectral coach.

a spectral coach is said to travel through the main street of the village. This stretch was once a regular route for old coaches, and phantom vehicles such as this seem to be embedded in the fabric of the place.

A similar journey is replayed at Rainham, on the outskirts of the Medway Towns, on the land where Bloor Place once stood. Christopher Bloor, who was considered a ladies' man, was murdered and decapitated by a group of local men, and his coach and horses, ridden by his headless form, can be seen gliding along the lanes.

In 1966, at Rusthall, in Hurst Woods, a man taking a stroll along a woodland path was startled by the galloping of a horse on the lane behind him. Turning to face the oncoming animal, the man was horrified to see a headless horseman dressed in Cromwellian battledress. The witness ran in terror.

A spirit is said to haunt Kemsing, which lies three miles north-east of Sevenoaks. Here a spectral knight on horseback gallops towards the church on 29 December each year. At Ball Lane, in Ashford, usually around New Year's Eve, a phantom horse-drawn carriage is heard to rumble along the lane and then crash. No one is sure if the spectral accident concerns a collision with a tree or if the carriage slides into a pond.

Phantom transport

Kent is littered with dark, eerie and remote roads. It is no wonder that these lanes are peppered with tales of phantom hitchhikers and ghostly accident victims. And inanimate objects, such as modes of transport, can also turn into ghostly phenomena. Take for instance the spectral limousine occasionally seen parked on the B2169 to Bayham Abbey, in Royal Tunbridge Wells. The car, which has been reported as black in colour, is said to shimmer and then vanish. A similar, or possibly the same, black car has also been observed at Bell's Yew Green. At Lamberhurst, a phantom bus has been reported around the town. For some reason the spectral vehicle travels along tight lanes, causing motorists to pull over suddenly. As the bus approaches, it vanishes!

A strange vehicle has been reported near the A25 by the fishponds between Seal and Borough Green, opposite Styants Bottom. A woman named Sue, from West Kingsdown, commented:

> I was out for a run and was passing the fishponds just as dusk fell, and saw a large white object moving down the hill towards the path in front of me. At first, I thought it was a small, white 4X4, until I realised that there was no sound, and also that the path was not wide enough for a vehicle at that point. I watched as the object carried on down the hill, and disappeared from my view behind a mound. When I got to the point that the object would have crossed the path I was on, there was nothing to be seen.

One of the most intriguing tales of phantom transport concerns a ghostly Spitfire plane which is said to appear every January over Biggin Hill. This location is reputedly haunted by several airmen, who have asked villagers directions before disappearing.

At Hawkinge, the sound of a Second World War aircraft has been heard regularly, despite the ghostly plane never showing itself. Several other witnesses to the phenomenon state that the sound belongs to a phantom German rocket known as a doodlebug. During the 1980s, a woman observed a phantom doodlebug over her home at Chatham. At Erith Marshes, there have been several reports in the past of a sound to suggest an aircraft has crashed. The ghost of a pilot has been reported in the vicinity.

A ghostly event is said to take place roughly every fifty years, relating to a great tragedy that took place on the Goodwin Sands at Deal. On 13 February 1748, the ship *Lady Luvibund*, owned by Captain Simon Reed, sailed from London to Oporto. Reed was accompanied by his bride, Annetta; their journey to Portugal was something of a honeymoon and their wedding reception was to be held below deck.

John Rivers, who in the past had attempted to take the hand of Annetta, was at the helm. It seemed as though the love rivals had sorted their differences, as Reed was quite comfortable with Rivers being his best man. However, things would soon turn nasty due to Rivers' deep-seated jealousy. As the boat reached the English Channel, Rivers attacked Reed with a club and killed him, then took control of the ship. The boat beached at the Goodwin Sands and, under the barrage of the high tide, all aboard were drowned. Rivers' mother testified against her son, claiming she had heard him state that one day he would get revenge on Reed.

Since the tragedy, a ghostly repeat has supposedly taken place, and the *Lady Luvibund* time and time again beaches on the Kent coastline. In 1798, it was alleged that the crew of the *Edenbridge* saw a three-masted boat heading straight for them. The captain of the *Edenbridge* acted quickly, steering his vessel away. However, as the other ship passed, it gradually faded into the mist. The *Edenbridge* steered back in the direction of the other ship but could find no trace.

Fifty years later, in 1848, again on 13 February, several ships in the area claimed to have seen the vessel, this time as it beached. Ships which sought the boat to give assistance could find no sign. Another fifty years after that ghostly recording, witnesses standing on the beach claimed they had seen a schooner with three masts beach on the Sands. There was no trace of the vessel.

The Goodwin Sands can lay claim to hundreds of shipwrecks over the years, the first being recorded in 1298, when an unnamed ship was lost near Sandwich.

A fairy sighting?

Joe Chester had a peculiar encounter in the late 1970s. He was at his Chatham residence with one of his daughters and one other person. Joe was sitting in his favourite armchair, chatting away, when suddenly he noticed a movement on the mantelpiece a few feet away. He stood up to get a better view, thinking an insect may have got into the room, and motioned to his daughter and the other witness. Joe was stunned to see a tiny humanoid figure lying down on the mantelpiece. It was pale in colour and immediately stood upright, measuring around 4in in height. It appeared to have no legs or arms, but did sport a pair of tiny wings which fluttered. The face appeared very human-like. Slowly, not wishing to startle the figure, Joe motioned to get his camera. One photograph was snapped before the entity began to hover; it glided, all the while remaining upright, across the room and then, once in mid-air above the sofa, it vanished. Sadly, when Joe developed the film, all that appeared on the image was a blur above the fireplace which had blotted out the flowery wallpaper.

To this day Joe Chester stands by his story, so maybe we can still believe in the magic of fairies residing at the bottom of our gardens.

The MP and the martians!

In the March 1998 issue of *UFO Magazine*, a Kentish mystery that would become known in UFO circles as 'The Burmarsh Incident' was exposed. It was made particularly high profile by the fact that it concerned the property of British politician Michael Howard.

The strange series of events began when reporter for the *Folkestone Herald*, Sarah Hall, telephoned local UFO group UFOMEK (UFO Monitors East Kent) – run by Chris Rolfe and Jerry Anderson – to report that on Saturday, 8 March 1997, at 3.30 a.m., she had seen a large triangular-shaped craft in the sky over Burmarsh. Sarah reported in 1998:

Joe Chester at his Chatham home, pointing to the exact spot where a fairy appeared.

I can still remember clearly the cold March night, when driving home from a friend's house in Romney Marsh, I was amazed to see a huge light in front of me. As I drove close I could hear a mechanical humming which, even recalling it now, some ten months later, still manages to raise the hairs on the back of my neck. Who knows what it was I saw, but the large pointed shape looming in the sky over a field near Donkey Street was not anything I had seen before, nor have I seen anything like it again.

The object shot off at great speed, and did this several times until it zoomed away into the night. Sarah described how the object displayed white and yellow lights around its edge, a circle of lights in the centre, and a bright light situated at each corner. An article was written for the *Herald* under the heading: 'The S Files – Herald reporter Sarah Hall tells the true story of the UFO experience everyone is talking about.'

A week or so after the sighting, UFOMEK received another report, this time from two firemen who said they had seen a similar object over the house of MP Michael Howard at East Kent. Although it was denied by Kent fire services, rather coincidentally a fire engine had been called out to Mr Howard's home at the same time as the UFO sighting. Also, within an hour of the sighting, there had been unconfirmed reports around Ashford, Lydd, Smeeth, Newchurch and Aldington.

Did a UFO buzz past the home of MP Michael Howard? (Image created by Neil Arnold)

The Kent County Constabulary were contacted via letter by Chris Rolfe and Jerry Anderson in reference to the sightings. Confirmation that the letters were received came from the Home Office and also a Kerry Philpott (Head of Secretariat Air Staff 2). After changing hands, a contact letter ended up in the possession of the Ministry of Defence. At the time, a reporter working for *Focus* magazine contacted the MOD, asking if they had any further information on the case, to which an official responded, stating categorically that there was no case or documents – despite the fact that they were in possession of Chris Rolfe's letter. Chairman of Kent Police Authority, Sir John Grudgeon, responded to a letter from Mr Rolfe by stating that there had been a minor security incident in the area which did not involve an aeroplane.

UFO Magazine, in covering the story, found that their investigations drew a blank and a year passed before the case took off once again. Jerry Anderson was visiting the Waterstone's book shop in Canterbury as UFO author Timothy Good was giving a talk there. It was here that Anderson was approached by a man who claimed that he was Michael Howard's neighbour, and that on the night of 8 March 1997, he and his wife were awoken by a disturbance at the MP's house. Men, resembling armed guards, were running to and fro, with some of them shouting commands. Above the house a helicopter was whirring, its searchlight scanning not the fields, but the sky!

Website The Why Files stated that, 'On 17 August 1998, Chris Rolfe received a letter from a certain Wing Commander A.W. Ward of the RAF, which included a warning to stop his investigations into a triangular object over Burmarsh, Kent.'

Although the paper the letter was typed on appeared to be official – it had an RAF header – the identity and whereabouts of Wing Commander Ward appeared to be a mystery. The Head of Secretariat Air Staff 2 took a look at the letter, and classed it as a forgery that should be sent to the police for further investigation as unsolicited mail.

Chris delved in deeper regarding the identity of the mysterious Wing Commander Ward, and found on record from 1991 an A.W. Ward who was listed as a squadron leader. When Mr Rolfe confronted him, he denied that the letter was from him but said that the signature was a very good replica.

Shortly after the incident, Anderson had his phone tapped, and he received a package which contained a cassette of Rolfe's telephone conversation with him discussing the Burmarsh incident. Sarah Hill also received a copy of the tape.

In UFO circles it has often been noted how witnesses of alleged unidentified flying craft, and those who research them, are 'monitored' or 'harassed' by persons unknown. This may simply be scare tactics – but ordered by who and why? Rumours of sinister agents working for persons unknown are rife within ufology. During the 1950s, such agents were known as MIBs, or Men In Black – well-dressed yet awkward and monotone individuals who seemed to turn up at the houses of UFO witnesses literally seconds after a sighting.

Naturally, such mysteries provoke paranoia and conspiracy theories. The authorities deny knowledge of such craft. What are they hiding? Are the majority of UFO cases covert military craft, or are the Ministry of Defence and the government aware of the existence of unexplainable objects in the sky, but unable to admit to such a presence in case hysteria ensues?

The late 1990s were certainly a busy time regarding sightings of anomalous craft in the skies of East Kent. During the March of 1997, at Ivychurch, a man walking his dog saw a prism-shaped object dart across the sky at incredible speed. On 7 March at Deal, between 5.30 and 6 p.m., a Barbara Kingcombe was strolling along Kelveston Road when she spotted an arrow-shaped object surrounded by flashing lights. It headed towards Margate. On 22 March, at Aldington, a Teresa Bridley awoke during a disturbed night and decided to go to the kitchen, but she was distracted by a large white object which glided beneath the glow of the moon. On 28 August, at Folkestone, at approximately 9 p.m., a Mr Jenkins looked out of his bedroom window to see a glowing, missile-shaped object perform strange circular movements before zipping towards the Channel. Three days later, a woman driving with her two children saw a cigar-shaped craft, orange in colour, moving towards her car. In 1998, Mark Watts, Member of European Parliament for East Kent, demanded an investigation after several sightings of UFOs in the Hythe area. The 'London Net' website reported the following:

He said that [there] were many independent sightings of strange flying objects in the weeks leading up to the General Election last May. They all occurred close to the home of former Home Secretary Michael Howard. When the MP stood for the Conservative Party leadership last summer, fellow Tory, Anne Widdicombe, made accusations that he had 'something of the night about him'.

East Kent seems to have had the highest concentration of UFO activity heading towards the millennium – but this may have been down to the Burmarsh mystery, which caused a snowball effect. At the same time, UFOs were reported regularly over Maidstone, Sittingbourne and Sevenoaks. None of these sightings were any more spectacular than reports of the past – take for instance the February of 1975, when over 300 schoolchildren and three teachers were said to have observed two strange aerial objects above their school at Strood. The objects were watched for more than fifteen minutes.

Waves of UFOs have emerged from the years 1954, 1960 and 1967; such sightings are nothing new. More recently, East Kent made the news when the *Independent*, on 20 October 2008, reported: 'Passenger jet's near miss with UFO above Kent.' It continued:

> A passenger jet coming in to land at Heathrow Airport in 1991 had a near miss with an unidentified flying object, according to newly-released Ministry of Defence files. The Alitalia captain was so concerned that he shouted 'look out' to his co-pilot after seeing a brown, missile-shaped object shoot past the airliner. The mysterious incident near Lydd in Kent was investigated by the Civil Aviation Authority and the military. Having determined that the object was not a missile, weather balloon or space rocket, the Ministry of Defence closed the inquiry and left the matter unsolved.

In 2009, literally hundreds of UFOs were reported in the skies over Kent. Website UK-UFO logged sightings of strange flying objects at Bromley, Ashford, Gillingham, Southborough, Maidstone, Canterbury, Swanley, Margate and Chatham. Although the majority were described as glowing, bright lights, one particular object, resembling a giant black triangle, was snapped by Google Earth off the coast of Thanet. The ominous shape has been dismissed as a camera blip, an insect, a boat or debris. The *Thanet Times*, 29 May, asked, 'What is mystery object off Thanet?' stating that the object, '... appeared on Google just off the coast between Kingsgate Bay at [*sic*] Botany Bay. The dark black object appears about 1,500 metres, nearly a mile, off the coast.'

The newspaper estimated the object to be more than 100m long. This story emerged after a similar object was seen off Ramsgate a week previous.

With avid UFO hunters concentrating their eyes on the skies for many years, it appears that these 'visitors' are not in any hurry to reveal their motive or secrets. Of all the paranormal mysteries, the UFO enigma is one that refuses to go away, and remains as peculiar as the day it was first noted, leaving more questions than answers.

The stick man & more Kentish curiosities

On the message board of the magazine *Fortean Times*, around 2003, there appeared a weird story posted on the 'It Happened To Me' section, which came from a chap residing at Loose Valley, two miles south of Maidstone. He reported:

In 2009, an ominous flying triangle was observed over Thanet. (Image created by Neil Arnold)

The following account is slightly shortened but otherwise unchanged and comes from my diary record for Tuesday 31 October 1978. Only the names have been changed.

We were all aged between 15 and 17 at the time.

'I will record a rather unpleasant experience which took place tonight. A group of about ten of us were sitting chatting in the Loose Valley at about midnight. After about forty-five minutes Will leapt to his feet slapping his head, saying there was a bee in his hair; he looked absolutely terrified. Both Dorothy and I saw the outline of a tall, thin figure wearing a hat dancing behind him. Will said later it was as if a terrifically loud buzzing was coming up through the top of his head. However, only Rachel heard any buzzing.

We partially satisfied ourselves that it must have been a bees' nest, and so we moved a little distance away. As we moved away Dorothy and I saw a ring outlined in the grass which enclosed where we had been sitting. Eventually it started raining so we headed for Rachel's house. As we left I turned around and saw the same thin black figure walk across the opening between the trees to where we had been sitting.

We had been sitting in Rachel's bedroom for a while, when I looked at Will who was reading and saw an amorphous black blob drop out of his hair onto the bed. I was the only one who saw this. A few seconds later a black shape started whizzing around. The main movement

BEWARE THE STICK MAN!

The 'Stick Man' of Loose Valley. (Illustration by Neil Arnold)

was from bottom left to top right as I was sitting, getting larger during the movement and inducing great fright. About four people altogether saw this.

Later the girls slept in a room together. Apparently Rachel and Molly saw the black blob in the curtains during the night. I, however, had an excellent night's sleep. On first awakening I saw the thin black figure silhouetted against the wardrobe doors.'

I have now moved away from the south-east but I occasionally meet Will. Even twenty years later he has been extremely unwilling to discuss the events of that night in any detail as he still found the memory disturbing.

Posted on the same forum was a report from an anonymous reader who claimed he had experienced a similar figure, which he called the 'black cut out man'. The sighting took place at Brockley, in the London Borough of Lewisham. The witness, who was with a friend at the time, noted how this thin, almost one-dimensional, figure approached them at six o'clock one morning and appeared to 'lollop' along. The witnesses fled in terror.

A cloaked figure, wearing a tall, dark hat and a glowing belt, was observed by two schoolgirls in 1961 at Keston Ponds, between Bromley and Biggin Hill.

The aforementioned Loose Valley harbours another strange legend, referred to in Roger Thornburgh's 1978 book, *Exploring Loose Village*. Speaking of All Saints' churchyard, he writes:

> On the south side of the church tower there are two table tombs, memorials to the Crispe and Penfold families who occupied Old Loose Court for many years. Just behind is a pillar memorial to the Charlton family of Pimps Court along Bushbridge Road. Its top is curved with three hideous faces, intended, so it is suggested, to frighten away the Devil.
>
> Tradition has it that if you stick a pin in the yew tree, run around it anti-clockwise twelve times (at midnight some say), and look in the small tower window above the Charlton memorial, you will see a face. Younger villagers add that what is seen is the missing fourth face from the top of the pillar. An older and much more macabre version of the story is that, having stuck a pin into the tree and run around it twenty-four times, you stand on the table near the tomb near the porch, look through the little trefoil window, and see a woman killing a baby. These fragments of folklore seem to be as near as we in Loose can come to having a resident ghost.

All Saints' churchyard at Loose.

The mysterious 'gargoyles' perched on the Holy Cross Church.

Holy Cross Church at Bearsted.

There is also a ghoulish paranormal legend from Bearsted church, which is situated three miles to the east of Maidstone.

In 1920, Charles Igglesden wrote:

Just below the parapet are several carved stone heads, some almost hidden in the ivy, but more remarkable are three large stone animals at the corners of the embattlements of the tower. Some good folk of the village will tell you that these are the figures of bears – naturally bears in Bearsted – and I have heard others say they are actually intended to be lions.

Either way, legend states that when the church clock strikes midnight, the stone creatures leap down from the church and seek food in the foliage of the churchyard. However, there is an extra twist in the fact that the church has no clock!

Alan Bignell, in his 1983 book, *Kent Lore*, simply comments:

On one night of every year the three jump down from the top of the tower, stretch their legs a bit on the green, and then always without being seen return to their perches to gaze over the surrounding roofscape with stony stoicism for another 365 days.

SELECT BIBLIOGRAPHY

Books

Arnold, Neil, *Monster! The A-Z of Zooform Phenomena* (CFZ Press, 2007)

Arnold, Neil, *Mystery Animals of the British Isles: Kent* (CFZ Press, 2007)

Beaney, S. & D. O'Leary, *Medway Towns* (Ottakar's, 2001)

Bignell, Alan, *Kent Lore* (Hale, 1983)

Chambers, Dennis, *Haunted Pluckley* (Denela Enterprises, 1984)

Devereux, Paul, *Haunted Land* (Piatkus, 2001)

Dixon, G.M., *Folktales & Legends of Kent* (Minimax Books, 1984)

Forman, Joan, *The Haunted South* (Jarrold, 1989)

Fort, Charles, *Lo!* (Gollancz, 1931)

Grebby, Jackie, *History of Pluckley* (? 1991)

Haining, Peter, *The Vampire Terror & Other True Mysteries* (Armada, 1981)

Harries, John, *The Ghost Hunter's Road Book* (Muller, 1968)

Hervey, Michael, *They Walk By Night* (Ace, 1968)

Igglesden, Charles, *A Saunter through Kent with Pen and Pencil* (Various)

Keel, John, *Strange Creatures from Time and Space* (Sphere, 1975)

McEwan, Graham J., *Mystery Animals of Britain & Ireland* (Hale, 1986)

Paine, Brian & Trevor Sturgess (eds) *Unexplained Kent* (Breedon, 1997)

Thornburgh, Roger, *Exploring Loose Village* (Loose Amenities Association, 1978)

Underwood, Peter, *Ghosts of Kent* (Meresborough, 1985)

Newspapers

Folkestone Herald
Gravesend Messenger
Gravesend Reporter
Kent Messenger
Kent on Sunday
Kent Today
Kentish Express
Kentish Gazette
Medway Messenger
Sheerness Times Guardian

Magazines

Bizarre magazine
Fate magazine
Fortean Times
UFO Magazine

Websites

Kent Big Cats www.kentbigcats.blogspot.com
Kent Online www.kentonline.co.uk
Medway Crop Circle www.medwaycropcircle.co.uk
Road Ghosts www.roadghosts.com
The Paranormal Database www.paranormaldatabase.com
The Why Files www.thewhyfiles.net
UK-UFO www.uk-ufo.co.uk
Village Net www.villagenet.co.uk

Other titles published by The History Press

Paranormal London

NEIL ARNOLD

With almost 2,000 years of continuous habitation, it is no surprise that the city of London can boast a fascinating array of strange events and paranormal occurrences. From sightings of big cats such as the Southwark Puma and the Cricklewood Lynx to the terrifying tales of the Highgate Vampire and Spring-Heeled Jack, along with stories of mermaids, dragons, fairies and alien encounters, this enthralling volume draws together a bizarre and intriguing collection of first-hand accounts and long-forgotten archive reports from the capital's history.

978 0 7524 5591 4

Haunted Kent

JANET CAMERON

Contained in this selection are stories of the hunchback monk at Boughton Malherbe, the black dog of Leeds, Canterbury's faithless friar and Dungeness' mysterious lady, as well as the famous tale of Lady Blanche of Rochester Castle. This fascinating collection of strange sightings and happenings in the county's streets, churches, public houses and country lanes is sure to appeal to anyone wondering why Kent is known as the most haunted county in England.

978 0 7524 3605 0

Haunted Canterbury

JOHN HIPPISLEY

A designated Ancient World Heritage site with numerous old landmarks, Canterbury is riddled with countless tales of ghosts and hauntings. From stories of the headless ghost of knight Hugh de Moreville, who was flung from his horse at Bridge, near the city, to the pump on Sun Street which reportedly produces red water, apparently marked by the blood of the martyred St Thomas Becket, this chilling selection of mysterious happenings will captivate anyone interested in discovering the ghosts of Canterbury.

978 0 7524 4998 2

Folklore of Kent

FRAN & GEOFF DOEL

Kent boasts a plethora of traditions which include hop-growing, smuggling and saints. It is bounded by sea on three sides, has the longest coastline of any English county and was the base for much maritime activity. This included trade and invasions, which gave rise to communities rich in sea-lore. This book also covers topics such as seasonal customs including harvest traditions; drama; witchcraft, saints and holy wells; and the background and songs surrounding fruit and hop-growing.

978 0 7524 2628 0

Visit our website and discover thousands of other History Press books.

www.thehistorypress.co.uk